DE
THE KEY OF
LIFE

LONG LOST
FOREVER
FOUND

Danny Baker Love

ONEIROS BOOKS

ONEIROS BOOKS

In association with
WWW.PARAPHILIAMAGAZINE.COM

First published in the world by ONEIROS 2014

ISBN 978-1-291-65466-0

www.paraphiliamagazine.com/oneirosbooks

Author's Statement / Maudlin Yet Sincere Acknowledgements

This, a collection of pieces culled from many a yesterday and the fear tomorrow's promise will actually be kept. Enjoy the journey from straight and narrow to all that jazz, fall from a cliff with the sheep or find a happy medium if you prefer- no boundaries. Just kidding- I've nothing against mutton.

Special thanks to Mark Hartenbach for shedding the light of dark possibility while excessively generous in giving time, thoughts-freely sharing the jazz wailing in a lion's heart.

Scotty, my brother...Adam (distant but never far, old fella)...the last of the ten ringers on my target...

Thanks to Dave Mitchell, Dire McCain and all at Oneiros Books and the Paraphilia Family (like the Manson's but crazy) for tireless efforts in making this book a reality and so much more.

Iris and Razor- Punk Hostage Press- with eternal gratitude for publication of my first book, FRACTURED. It doesn't end there.

S.A. Griffin for friendship, continued support and plentiful imparted wisdom.

Richard Modiano, Dennis Cruz, Apryl Skies, Rich Ferguson - not exactly sure how to express my thanks, but this page would feel woefully incomplete without your names on it.

PB- Could it be, my Muse, that we will finally sail across the universe together in the boat that came to rescue us?

The girl I left behind a decade ago- you know who you are and why, M- timing's everything, huh?

A shout out to family, the TNT Crew and anybody who's encouraged discouraged footprints anywhere.

To all who have seen in me what I sometimes don't- those who've graciously presented me in their work and extended invitations to their events or pushed for my inclusion and recognition. The list is long and any attempt to quantify it would certainly come up short.

Finally, though among the most important pieces of this, the riddle wrapped enigma-dog pissing on the whole absurd ovoid conundrum from a dirty water cart- the amazing medical triumvirate- Scott, Sean and Andy. If ever one wishes to be shrunk, exsanguinated or electrocuted, I'd highly recommend their services. Who'da thunk I'd still be here to rattle cages while listening to the bats in my guano head war with one another- often almost pestilent as the human race? Thanks Docs.

Introduction

in this present day world of tame, dumbed-down, derivative, throwaway culture there are few artists creating genuine in the moment. fortunately we have writers like danny baker who slice through barbed-wire banality. he fans the flames of intuitive stream-of-consciousness in the grand tradition of henry miller, nealcassady&thelonious monk.

there is no 'technique' to this kind of creation other than to give the muse reign. let the mind roam free. there are seemingly illogical turns of phrases that jerk the reader's head from the relative comfort circular thought. in quoting gut-bucket bluesy homespun then swerving off the charts intellect that takes the monster to new heights, there's a surrealist quality to the work though i would never slap that to the page. his work can be densely abstract for a few lines then socked into absolute clarity-impressionistic word salads stripped of acknowledged definitions.

baker improvises behind a strange soundtrack that seeps through border radio static while wielding unquestionably superior vocabulary. poetic bombs scatter any allusions to literary theory- operating beyond the realm of ordinary consciousness as well as communication yet plaster ivory with shards of essential information that will open the perceptive reader to infinite possibility in each click.

there is no contingency plan or predictable outbursts here. there is no public spectacle imposing one way out on bewildered audience. hyper-paranoid nerve collage rifles through the pockets of time- going for the throat of the herd mentality while slipping contributions to needy individuals.

white-fisted fingers on ribbed wheel braced for inevitable wild ride that lays down pure inspiration without looking both ways for supposed criterion.

each piece in this series of prose poems works for me on several levels. i suspect the reader will find several of his/her own. ushering in understated murmuring, yes- along with clamorous verbosity. lionized burning questions lie side by with raw sacrificial lambs. dialectics of soul deep in hand to hand combat with at times uncooperative chemistry.

never grandstanding though certainly capable of poetic knockout. slapping dispassionate into a month of next sundays. planting black flag on unsettling fault line. dressing down archetypes that don't hold up their end of the bargain. slinging revelatory blueprint for deconstructing geometrical whammy.

baker unleashes the beast on literal translation & adamant caricature, trippy numskulls & mercenary hearts. sharpening hoodoo curvature with samurai determination. touching on occasional reference point before nimbly moving on to unchained/uncensored. scattering loaded dice across ever-expanding radius.

quoting artaud-baker is writing his way out of hell. a world of psychological pain, remorse, bitterness- fearlessly challenging staid language & biological fallout from institutional imbalance.

possessing uncanny ability to piece together bone-crunching carved-in-stone with 180 degree non sequiturs that assimilate entire piece- but only on its own terms. he creates vernacular from metaphoric state of altered idiom.

this is a world where textbook versions & absolute absurdity collide violently. a cyclone sweeping so-called sign of the times to meticulous tabula rasa. ambiguous concepts whistle through abandoned bone yard. unabashed sings praises of drop-dead beautiful muse.

surfing shudder at the very thought on wave of zeitgeist. cinematic detail jackknifes into animated over-the-top. voluminous desire to throw it all down a hunch- occasionally leaning hard on disputed. overactive imagination is an oxymoron.

personally i think this book is the future of poetry. it's never too late to treat yourself to some truth. you'll find that & so much more in danny baker's art. you have my word.

mark hartenbach

Master Of No Universe

Put the bottle on the table. Follow with your pistol. You'll need it. Actually something bigger but beggars can't be choosers. Records skip. Songs end abruptly. As will yours. As eggs will hatch, so angels get wings. A train-wreck approaches the horizon. The engine rumbles close. You see glitter- unable to face the music in all its minor reverberations. The rocks care nothing of burden. Hold no candlelight vigils for landslide victims of their own success cum failure. A torrential downpour reigns your parade. Center of the universe. Master. Neither apply. Destiny's raven cackles a wicked squawk. Your press envelopes your all. You are your press. Your press is you. You are he smote whom was first made king. Golden child of his own consciousness snaps neck, news at eleven. Dancing secretaries stream halls. They seem to be shrinking- the halls. It's nothing more than illusion brought to bear in shadow of a gargantuan cranium expanding at terminal velocity. High on your scent- secretaries retch in disgust. As the mail roomer. As the janitor. As the journeyman pro you screwed out of bonus after devouring his starfucking wife. Maybe not though once broken, lines rarely regain their straight and narrow. You dance too close for government work. Oxymoron notwithstanding. Your tune is unintelligible. You're out of tune. You are a toon. You need a tune up. She had suicidal tendencies- your mommy. I saw her and your mommy's dead. Crushed under a shiny new bulldozer bearing your name in silver flake. I saw a seagull. He offered me some of his bony fish meal. You shoot seagulls for sport. Depositing remains beneath your insecurity. The record's skipping again. A glance in your bottle reveals dwindling sands. Sound engineer seems to be fading your vocals. Grab your pistol. The reaper's coming. Death rock parts sky only you see. Plentiful distortion couples with bone mangling bass- only you feel it as your endoskeleton rattles. The track's laid down. Few questions remain. Wuchu gonna do with that pistol? You're outta ammo and not much of a marksman to start. Spray and pray- your life philosophy. Tough going when the other cowboy kicks his spurs with ice veins dead set on making you dead. An albatross joined seagulls protesting your very earthly presence, crapping over a parking lot. Your car alone is hit. Repeatedly. Wuchu gonna do with that pistol? Never bring a handgun to a gunfight. Never fight a land war in Asia. Not applicable of course, but while we're on the subject of prohibitive axiom, why not mention it? With finality of your days approaching, what is it you still hide? Seems you are many. Is that the secret? So many pagoda faces. All look alike. Yeah, it's prejudiced. Sue me. And please pray tell, what *is* your name? Yeah, you told me. Trivial nonsense tends to skip memory more rapidly these days. Blame the liquid paper. Oh that's right. You're your press. Your press is you. Meet the press. Steam engine meet press. Meet you. You are your press. Turn out the lights, the party's over. No- not it. That train's on the wrong track. Coup d'état- ticket to ride this jerk-fest. Center of all universal planes tossed to margins like chum to a white shark. Yep your dirge passes before your eyes with a throaty growl. Splat. Guess it was the right track after all. Turn out the lights... but first, a last question: can i have your pistol?

I'll take that as a yes.

Toe-Dip Into Broken Lines

They make you feel small. Their profundity wrapped in riddle-tangled in metaphor's web. An enigma requiring all faculties and some not possessed to uncover. Superfluous flowers stealing blood from theme and reader. Burying you in dictionary tome. Tomb soon to follow. Time is of the essence. Written in the sky is begging for mercy and a simple explanation. Uncovering the point is the point though seems so pointless. *A garden requires an occasional trim.* Certainly not the most scholarly poetic but easy enough to grasp, no? Don't look too far beneath the words or you'll miss the tip of the spear. Everybody loves the rapture of melodious letters forming a new horizon to envision and upon which to dream. That- of course and until the letters choke themselves, strangling song burgeoning from heart. Taking center stage. And the actors are invisible behind the pedantic curtain. And the audience is left struggling for comprehension of the black-lit scene while exit music plays and theater lights signal it's time to go. A commodity not to be taken lightly hasn't the resource to weather the storm of archaic. The audience leaves feeling small. Writing maudlin rave reviews for a play to which even the author cannot attest. A quill delights chanting devious- pounds keys afar further obfuscating the plot. Perchance that's the aim in itself for the eggs being scrambled have been on the stove for something greater than thousands of fortnights. Vapid word demands a blanket to keep warm. Magic does lay behind the hefty obscure when organic. What's organic anymore anyway? I have been given that answer but it's too crowded a house to take seriously. Anything but Monsanto is too thinly veiled. A horse-carriage of wobbly wheels with shiny hub caps. A trapper's black hole with foliage roof hiding its bloodlust. Glossy gold flake atop primer atop bondo. I could continue but I'd hate to be misunderstood. Often misinterpreted is here committing seppuku. Of course you don't feel small. Wiki's got your back. Hara-kiri just revealed its birth name. But you knew that already. A mirror stands before me as I inscribe this page with opacity- obtuse abstraction bordering surreal nothingness. But then that's the point, you understand. And of course you understand. How not, given that you live in my head and me yours? And I've got a bridge for sale. See me about it. But you get it, right? Or do you just feel small, seeking meaning beneath wax paper shamboozlery? I could have just said *trim the garden just a wee bit* and saved us all the time. Though again- what fun the interpretive head scratch dance in the orchestra pit? And in writing my own reflection, I feel small however that was the target. Seems I hit it. Did you hit yours? Or do you just feel a bit lesser, shedding the weight of sequel under cover of darkness and Oxford?

Shrinking Chasm

It's dawning on me like revelation though it's nothing new. Cast in a die of eternal damnation delivered by reflection in a still pool. Not able nor willing to see, let alone grab the rescue line. Quarreling ducks land- ripple the pond's glass surface- further distort the answer which seems to be in failing health. More so with passing time. Question pulls a ticket for a line of no end. Jackhammering a tar spotlight so many years. Left to rot in my own somber devices. Clarity is duct taped. A crater drags me to its trough- closes lead curtains for winter, disregarding June moon which isn't a proper Asian noun. Curling in fetal position does little to aid. Evading splash of holy water and deadly light of day. Chasm is too large to bridge dead dreams. Though still grasping at short straws some might call hope. Knowing better yet still drawing breath. Perhaps I'll come to discover sense to it all- why the wicked bury the righteous. And in some unexpected seismic shift find satisfaction in comprehension. Admittedly the longest shot on the board. Hope springs eternal for the hopeless. The horses will still run races only to finish precisely where they started.

Saturday Abstract

Heart of the matter is ticking asymmetrically. Tipping balance to a number asymptotically banging against negative infinity. Reprobate gaspipe smokers bouncing about dressed as clowns, decrying success- real, ostensible, earned and un. Hate clowns. Hopped up on heavy hits of jealous barley. Waxing self adulatory with pride of explorers over that long discovered- released in sweat of thousands of inebriated years. Millions. Only to be narc'd back into line circulating definitive ends of forgotten. Drunkards selective in memory find wall melt uncertainty floating in one too many. One too many dogma declarations swirling in a pint of a million undulating atoms plus some. Rally. Rail. Bound stoned naked across the avenue. Take the street. It peaked ages ago. Coastal dream on mescaline mesa. Worthless. Immune to new high. Death pends all in her fold. Dance light on self diagnosed humanist certified graves. Wavy sod reverses course. Lifeguards drown. Misanthropic dons many a vest. Colors flickering iridescent stoplight. Crash- cars and trucks in motion and idle. Horse drawn carriage leaves scene of last lynching. Shifting tide of paper constituencies constant. Expedited reporting high on crystal. Palms still stagger in air- albeit more fetid. Nothing changed but rate of change. I'm dancing to fall of empire. Simple two step. Never forgotten. Promises to be same as its lineage- decline. Perhaps faster. Repeat though it is. It shall. Reporting, vapid. History, purview of sobriety. We're torched. Wasted to point of I told you so. Just forgot what it was i said in a plume of lemongrass extract.

Snowy Channel To The Cosmos

Eyes tumble in blackened sockets. Scramble as brains on terminal neglect. Patter of feet of no shoe flee thuggery of slummin' it turned marketing ploy. Nubile genuflect for entrance where haggard once roamed, wild ones. Broken sight, shattered dreams. Deconstruction. Reconstruction. Devolution. The bird eats. Ragged puke fortified bile. Young lose youth. Semblance of chivalry dusty in hidden corners of iniquity. Empathy served thin like butter. Familiar black boots approaching- battle hardened tin deserving rep. Scatter avoidance best bet. Dilated pupils glisten Scooby Doo, talkin' loud. March about beneath disregarded character. Roaming days to blur atop altered history. Verity and reinvention running together like coital fluid without climax. Cults birthed under stars undisturbed by Franklin and Edison. Starfucking denial an old creature. Staggering rearranged dreamscape delusion. Fear, loathing. Then blessed darkness. Escape to shadow. Marbles constrict to light. About the day, that's it. And tumbling eyes burning sockets to void all around.

Slapping A New Vein

Optimism runs for cover of invincibility. Preferable is head in sand- undeniably running risk of missing rendezvous point but I'd lay odds on destructive devices dotting the course and finding missing points misses them entirely. Like fight for life in a tornado. Search swirl debris for an econ 101 diamond/water paradox wrist watch of life affirmation less than a Bangkok lap dance. Outta control centripetal sucking into the vortex of tilt winged possessions owning you. Most valued, worth least. Accompanying, a choir of frantic moo's. If even your dog cares, luck rains your parade. Followed stars south. Now on first name basis with exile from up high. Spins a child's delight-giggles malevolent. Illuminating roads toward seeming easy street, ephemeral if not altogether illusory. Lighted paths head-on smash-t-bone pawn shop humility. Peer under every bed for horned monster. Slippery this, expectation. Want none of it. Still being treated. Irradiating microscopic remnant tumor of hope. Prayed to a clay statue of frozen tear, spiked headdress. Hecho en Shanghai. Effigy of I've no time for your banality. Opium buzz disappears in vapor. 'Twas but momentary lapse in judgment wrought by weight of degenerating introspective, this spiritual experiment. If only so easy. Gazing into paradise light. Dig a hole, dig. Do a headstand. Fill in hole. No regrets. Just mud-cake and answers lost in wind of the day's sectarians-these, cud chew karma handbag toters. New opium for a new world. Sorry, can't find that vein.

Walk

Faceless heads polka dot hallowed ground now hollow. Charm took character on extended vacation, pining for greener pasture. Summerbugs fly sorties entropic under artificial rays of light blocking galactic brilliance. Labradors lick wind- crap organic. Biodegradable shit bags fill transient up and comers' dumpsters. Shit in more honest sections stays where laid. Never been pissed tosses jagermeister. Hoping to get laid secures her black mane- act not the least selfless. Young love tongues- banks credit before old debts set in. Nine to five jog away the numbs. Dilated coffee crowd argues politics. Bloodbath ensues while fighting to make same point. Vishiswa genetically enhanced served warm with a side of cold rabbit-chew. Tequila scratches her prius- fumbles for right key on wrong chain- crashes sector car. Heavy dogs stop barking. Whimper instead. Aging with alacrity pushing sound barrier. Arches fallen flat as widget sales. Store signs pop from ground floor of sterility constructed, largely vacant. Blend to sea of impressionistic who gives a fuck. Broken wander ground-stare aimless. Telltale what happened written all over faces not yet resigned. Wrong end of gun points at never to blossom hard ridden. Nosering and vet rumble drunk over handout space no better than that kitty corner. Faceless fade the scene as dark peaks. Chopper roars daddy complex past no return. Cruisers set nav systems for home James. I perspire summer towards bed. Sweet success wafts from post war blocks of medicinal. Tumble tired steps to front door. Full circle. Dog wag tail, certain grass is greener inside.

She's Gone

Fields of green lay untended. Disinterested tap-dances fuck-me pumps on white superdome- digs heels in. A full plate overflows. Voices surround in a bubble. Seem frantic though unintelligible. Leave me writhing pit-gut attempting to ascertain source or meaning- latter patent nonsensical. And sweetly aromatic grasslands lay untended, extending a come hither gesture. Disdainful heels dig deeper, no longer disinterested but unequivocally opposed to discovery. Pomegranate passages follow each door opened. Ignorant masses don't always appear blissful. Informed never do. Pagoda mathematics torture them. Voices argue among themselves. Distortion cranked to eleven. Deaf to their meetings, hip to their decisions by necessity. Crack their rules like quake to pavement daily. Hopping fences to fresh distraction. Aging luggage in tow though marginally lighter at the moment. Over the fence ain't a cakewalk. Sandman blasts death rock upon exhausted pied piper of can't let it go. Awake to mountain of lost bags, some dew soaked cud to chew on awhile. And forever pit-gut in stagnant pond of misunderstood.

Catch And Release

Retreat to a safety net wasn't dealt today. Maybe it'll fall in the river though gambling on the last card kills more Jews than Hitler. A charge headlong into a new day overstates the condition most dawns. By looks of things a slow trot would be more accurate. Hormonal whitewater run to familiar though uncomfortable depths. Devil I know's as much a bastard as the one I don't. Unconvinced there's one I've yet to meet. Shadow warrior beneath dreams both caviar and blood. Block wall's crumbling. Connecting dots. Salting the pepper. Listening for trumpets signaling an end to hemispherical infighting. Completed foundation for whole. Construction delays persist. No horns to blow soon. Itching for sated, I gut a beluga. Devour unborn. Chase it with slash-wrist. An outlaw, did both without permit. Needing a club, draw ace of spades. Gargantuan waste of the perfect card. Discarded black rose yet to bloom. Toss it back to the river.

Adhesive

Another voice. Well same really but with nascent rasp. And it's hers and she's displaying lands distant and confusing with colors of rainbow I've yet to see and odd boundless expansion of viscera. Not unique, though few may hear me and those typically pre-date my struggle. Formatting time waste and contemplation of structure. She calls in her order and none includes definition nor organization. Despises separatist label. Poetry. Prose. Prose-poetry. Short. Narrative. Memoir. Fiction noir. Novel. Hard to gather to where I'll be led next. Down what endless road of unknown. Into which claustrophobia. Behind door to shrinking hallway hosting more party guests than expected. Or maybe the right amount. I've been known to exaggerate numbers where too many pulse raisers trespass under misanthrope gray. Certain not to sanitized is flight plan. Voices fly free as glue mist adhering to cortex. Not wet sea, that of sand nor ocean of tar and granite will lose them. She approaches, seeking word-song. Sounds like a request for alliteration in a dozen tercets. Quick witted, she chuckles-knows none will arrive. Today it's chef's menu. Prix fixe. Meat cooked to taste, bloody or raw. Hastily arranged with no garnish.

Off The Subject- Stupid Wants To Play Too

Ever have a bad dream? I mean something brutal…like a mullet in parachute pants and gold chains blindly stumbling your way in haste and waste post happy hour on Friday night outside the times square subway station through a torrential storm of foot, elbow and ass and in desperation you try avoiding contact if for no other reason than out of fear of contracting acute flock of seagulls or a bad case of Okie retardation and finding yourself waking in a cornfield the next morning. In full stride, Don Johnson approaching - pastels, loafers with no socks and a Kenny Loggins cassette in a fucking Walkman as you strut down fifth performing a Footloose number aloud unaware- deafened by the bright yellow headphones, paralysis dictates no matter how hard you try, you can't avoid him-legs wobble non-compliant, and as you're bumped by a Jamaican whangdoodle replete with bad teeth and good weed, a genie flies out of the steamy crack of the subway's ass and before you know it, the cassette's moved on to Danger Zone and you tear up, crying for goose, begging a couple of donuts with billy-clubs to arrest you for killing your friend, while freely admitting you took Meg out for a tail spin and close fly-by only hours before splashing her husband's brain all over the inside of his fucking helmet and your F14 somewhere over bumfuck while demanding to know who was gonna clean your plane, simultaneously audibly wondering aloud the whole time how he ever got into the navy in the first place given his prodigious teen drug habit and close personal relationship with Jeff Spicoli, then getting showered with more champagne genie flake and realizing you're walking into J P Morgan's packed main branch office at lunchtime, naked but for the Walkman, Kenny Loggins, and a pulsating hard-on? Yeah, me neither…just wondering…

Lonely Pedestal

Tenuous spans constructed. In ill advised word, embryonic gap is expanding crevasse, increasingly susceptible to ravages of further separation. Termites dine on faux pilings. Rescue rope is but a wick. And in our writings. Expression predictably monotheistic. Inviting grin offers enlightened path to so called community. Itself a contrivance- by definition omit those unprepared for hijack to common sentiment. Who would choose instead standing tall laughing in gale headwind. Smiling enlightenment frightens me to no end. Unilaterally ratified platform proclaims word sacrosanct- proceeds to delineate which word that is. Closes door on novel approach. On outside looking in again. Seeking immunity deal from vagary of loathe-stoking virus charge. Well, separation anxiety is mostly though not uniformly echo, anyway. Bridges, ash. Eviscerated by those self elected to lay the foundation. An irony none too comforting though none too surprising. Remuneration, a life supply of kindling and at least one scribbling infidel for the stake-fry. Traitor to the cause. Unwelcome lone flag in the cemetery of a thousand poets resting atop ash of unapproved olive branch. Razed to stated ends severing ties to unwelcome in order to avoid violent penetration. Dissent, a goal in name alone. Not surprising when intransigent agitator mysteriously fall under buses. Court of popular opinion authorizes shove when life or limb or prearranged tenet are at risk of violation or misperceived such. McCarthy's risen. Are you now or have you ever been a traitor to utopia? To best of your knowledge, is Judas in your family tree? I enter highway via off-ramp. My weather vane crows counterclockwise, ship lists. Grinds eye to eye with rogue wave crosshair. On the bow, I piss in the wind. No one ever hears. I piss louder, senator. Next question. Fuck it. I take the first.

Fool

Half way through this endeavor (low case endeavor) though declarative statements lead to virulent hoof in mouth. Typical, this odyssey looks to have twins or triplets. Trippin' to far off galaxies with sunrise perspective and modified take on subjects at hand. Objects perhaps more aptly or as well. English phlunked bong load hellucinajin and betwean. Actuarial had me offed five years back. Adjusted for hormonal imbalance said give or take twenty. Figure it could give me fifteen. Arithmetic comes easy though could be entranced by tarot and crystal. Might be gypsy cards saw straight. Well, give or take twenty. Sort of legit underwriter, product of a chance bump in the night- well degreed and certified is yet less optimistic though smiles Cheshire type- his employer didn't write a policy. Shredded aspiration has me reckless. Ripping straight through infrastructure, china shop bull like. Circumspection all but eggplant. Roughly translated that means something on the lines of: stuck on red smear octagon concrete in full view. Bearing invisible mass inside my guard. Eating invisible fist and elbow. Apparition, always best fought at arm's length. Hidden opponent is likely reflection or friend, broadly defined. Double jab some distance. Useless is loving demons not loving you back. Angels ain't no better, adorned in flaming haloes- flash a debutante furtive glance. My balance is only in their war. Unfortunate is love's declaration, inevitably reneged upon and etched in the wall of recollection. Life incarnate spits quite a load itself. Some things just take a fool's age to acquire. Like the age we realize what fools we are and have always been.

Raining Again

Hold your water. Hold mine too. Stuck perpetually tangent to crossroad of don't give a rat's ass and nothing. I could just piss. You can buy it or simply call it rainfall of pungent beginning and end. Most seem easily fooled by malicious detail in fine print. The rest want so badly, judgment and self-preserving instinct are launched on newspaper schooners. What results- drowned expectation. Selling sand to Arabs has been banned by homeland security and Inuit ice sales have plunged into the arctic. Doubloons cascade down the mountain with bad intent, crushing base camps indiscriminate. Smoldering dialectic has none but itself to spar with. You could buy the two face dogma or just realize piss down the neck isn't rainfall and opposing mugs are but one juxtaposed against the other. A frightening unholiness, this prismatic handshake and wink between professed adversaries. Coin flip conspirators aren't much concerned whether any sees the ungodly union. Bargain nobody sees beyond the yellow brick façade and velvet curtain which fronts their terror. They're only half right which is half wrong. Who are not blind are selectively ignorant. Pretend not to feel the micturition for what it is. From desperation comes hopeful sense-neglect. Crap, just pissed down my own leg. Let's call it rain. I'm numb, remember...and don't give a rat's ass.

Rest Not In My Healing Hand

Evil sits behind chart and stethoscope, playing Jim Croce on a mirrored tuning fork. "Enter slug, this realm of do no harm...to my practice. Front door beckons my exit, though I'll indulge you. Pulse races. Mine that is. I've family to dismember like gutted steer. Not sure of your problem or why it should concern me. Wear a neck brace when typing or playing slap-happy on your mistress or pool-boy, whatever your thing. Take this signature to the victim employing your sorry ass. Take your insurance card and first born to reception. Take a hike. I'm taking break. These three day weeks conspire to be the death of me. And damn it all, the constant chatter of semi-lucid eats at me, sticking around even when I punch holes through human silhouette targets at a hundred yards. Truth be told, it serves as good motivation, keeping aim true. What's this? Not your chart, you say? See my initials? M.D. Majordomo. Dr. Majordomo. Refer to previous directions. I'm him. Capital H. Just ask me. I bleed for universal sin. I'm tenured. You're just sick. What say you is more pressing than my health at this very moment? Certainly not your sickness. You can afford to absorb virus, even death. These things happen to no macro negative. What though, if medical legend such as myself shall be stricken? Who will provide no care then? And with all this overbearing universal weight and responsibility cast upon me to boot. You see my conundrum, right? Yeah, you're alright. Here's a bottle of all's well with the world. Now take that aforementioned hike. Don't tell anyone of the all's well with the world. Can't have compassionate in my public records. Someone may get the wrong idea. Can't stomach it, forced to examine infirmed. Gives me the willies. What a lowly place for a man of my education, don't you think? So very far beneath me. Don't figure for a moment though that I don't care. Of course I do. Workers comp pays workers' docs pretty fucking good. Yeah, how about that! From this, DC steals their piece, using it to tie my intestines until peritonitis sets in. Still, you lucked out. I've many a deduction. It would reflect quite poorly upon you were things such that I had to upsize my superego in the name of better patient care or something of that type inanity. One can't be too hard on oneself and expect satisfactory results, no. Anyway, I'm glad we spoke I must admit- a rarity. I really can see your points. Here's an extra bottle of feel-good. See, this type charity? Were I to fall indisposed, who would remain to show none but the lawyers? Besides, rumors from inside the bar(s) indicate a lynching of one their own will take place on a reformatory yard in attempts to thwart plans laid out by some quirky Englishman in certain moments of clarity related to ancient Rome or some such prehistoric jungle. Smart money's on her majesty's quirk. The peasants won't settle for but one. Yes, you have good points. Glad you opened up. See the receptionist on your way out. I've long violated the oath with you. This extraneous dialogue you seem intent on continuing is impacting the books, harming the practice. Leave now. Your blabbering is costing time. I've other patients to avoid. They pay too."

Eight Ball And Faithless Dirge

I see light. Light frightens me. Like most proclivity, a revelation anything but informative. Consulting expert- grabbing the magic eight ball, child safe kind. Jaundice eyes sunken in stuffed purple bags dart for shaken conclusion, always landing on "don't count on it." Ambiguous as tentative sky, but pretty much sets up the next act- ergo rarely disappoints. And must submit, a substantive improvement over "it is decidedly so." Creator of diamond dream outed as zirconia nightmare one day beyond return deadline. Didn't take long- losing faith in the latter prognostication. The astute orb ceases the joke upon learning the cat fled the bag. Like the parrot, knows more of his report than previously believed. Licking wounds suffered when still adequately naïve to seek expert counsel and ubiquitous coat-tail wicked droll twenty steps removed from now. Feet are soaked in shattered remnants of plastic fate swimming with twenty possibilities. With each passing moment I know less than the preceding. An unequivocal inevitability, however- like flame-out meteor, your expiration date came and went. You'll never lie again. I slip into dark Atheist and howl victory at the orange crescent moon. A tear drops through wanting lips. In the distance, a like howl. The accompanying sobs linger like a dying bagpipe.

Invisible Hand

Embedded in psyche wrought with disconnect. A scepter-constant reminder Greek rulers make bad lovers and kingdoms expensive. Normally disclosure too late to escape landslide gold flake empire promising nirvana. Crumbling-mined ore held up by quicksand democracy- utopia stared into a puddle, obsequiously distorted snapshot. Bone ash and shame litter landscape of abject veracity. Dis-redacted text reveals dystopian vessels beneath veneer. Carpe diem requests are now mandatory before seizing anything- applications processed within a six month window give or take a year. Ambition dies as I speak. In firm hold of the invisible monster- tentacles constricting at each level in every capacity. Us, prey- victims of malodorous addiction to want of immediate satisfaction promising agonizing paranoia yet ostensible trappings pull too hard to abstain. Vitamin B and Mannitol cut with just enough real to keep traffic. Us, junkies enticed to our ends by swords we voluntarily yield. Comatose monkeys with mainlines pushing the button 'til heart gives. Lab rats torturing ourselves into maze frenzy at the smell of cheddar dichotomy not difficult to grasp when viewed in context though deciphering encryption still leaves me feeling vulnerable like invisible doom sits above awaiting just the right moment.

Beware Of Owner

The dominoes fall in writhing snake dance precision. Tumble to horizontal mediocrity. Level playing field on all fields is solid human interest story but loses viewership after a season. Viva la difference went the way of sunset hookers, lawn darts, lard fries, lead paint and asbestos- a few of my favorite things. Offensive interference is killing my buzz but never gets jailed. A no trespassing sign demands penalty for failure to heed though plugging Jehovah's ain't legal. I coat my house in high fructose corn syrup to keep out the riff-raff. Posted a sign. Deceptively lowering same if prerequisite of lascivious escapade with comely granola lass. Otherwise, bell doesn't ring. And for the love of all things beautiful, I associate with none who would fail to keep rapidly draining attention and years deceased patience. The mirror fogs. No matter, vertical I am or so fool myself. A séance with Freud left me believing a third of my psyche is working overtime- further fogging the mirror. Who am I to argue?

Smoke On The Barter

Holy smokes. Up in smoke. Actually down in it. Burning out on burn out. Slack back stumble about. Ink fades in light of day. Hard exterior. Endo-system prepares for collapse. Danger is a man perceiving no point. Glaring a mile through whatever confronts. No range is safely roamed by the excessively aware. Replete with pyrotechnics unseen but for the knowledge they lay in wait. Physicists tear into the equation. Astronomers ask the stars. Shrinks channel Jung. Existentialists pit Camus against Dostoyevsky while savoring the great digitally enhanced simulated splitting hares. Tastes like chicken. Lacking patience for other than timely reply, I just tug on twisted hemp paper, well endowed. Could be effect of utter boredom. Would nap on it but I'm burnt. Instead, cogitating the riddle in full Tommy Chong. Not unbiased, but it'll have to suffice.

Intolerant

I've regaled exploits of galactic travel without ever departing N. America. Fleeting endorphin and dopamine calm truncated by a torrent of opposing evil clones. Bouts of adrenaline-thrust blistering scenery already baked in Ra's occasionally overbearing benevolence which never strikes me as charitable. Cowering paralyzed in the face of the monster. Battling friend and foe equally as my standards have overgrown my tolerance. Swooning in grips of rainbow and writing on walls only a dose or a few thereof can see. Green wood spillin' dice where dicey is. Wide eyed pessimist seeking what for after tripping on Tzu's path. Find interesting though somehow empty relief in the quest. Curved back straightened only to return its rightful place. Chipping teeth gnaw themselves. That much never took a break but a couple hours for ten martini lunch dates. All of which might be no more than a dishonest stab in the dark. Just hope the dark doesn't stab back.

Tarnish

Informal discussion with silver lining inevitably ends in a carnage scene. Like Lancelot staring at disloyal impressed upon tarnished armor with a life its own. Apocryphal metal striking in resemblance to real deal. Stabbing at sin with jaundice eye through wine and roses liver. Silver lining can be forgiving though rarely displays itself despite innocuous even reassuring codename. Glory is a double edged sword. That thrust into our own at each crossroad with objective introspection run amok. What topples the gilded castle on the hill. Splinters round table of ego. Like a tall proud mount from which we've yet to fall to realm of indisposed phoenix. An implement of death plunged through chaste archetypical moralist by his own hand in what is perhaps an existential punishment or simply an acknowledgement that human sometimes ain't good enough.

The Garden

Atonement, a speck on the calendar. Transcendent, the sin. Unsure transgression-sunsets and dawns on ancient maps- evicts poison from soul. Were belief to drip into subconscious as a faucet leaks would statute of limitation absolution suffice for dangling participle? No line stems, rendering moot the rhetoric. To revisit when aunts drop testicles as hell freezes over. Lack of inertia treads lightly on the world outside. Either direct result of age and health or divine intention to limit new trespass in order to catch hindsight penance sometime prior to the checkered flag yet with hope, a hop skip and jump after a final shot of gratuitous mischief. Shame is discarded talent. Mayhem sledgehammers keys for now though deflates, slowly obscuring breadth of antisocial proclivity. Slowly is a projectile whose arc is defined by one's chronology. Lifetime, a nano-tick on a three thousand year clock. Repentance, a repetitive scene in a screenplay buried once a year by actors antsy cuz the brisket is delayed 'til after sundown. Bite into a mid-day apple. The snake nods reassuring.

Altamont

Foreboding backdrop. Scepter sits above the mass. Stage sets
dark energy. Rolling sod awaits rockslide. Death's head patrols,
fed by a well of no visible bottom. Mood intentionally
manipulated ominous spook. Disrespect sits uninvited on prized
steed. Fuel burns cowboy to action. Rollicking lines bunker in.
Advantage, purview of the black knight. Ugly is an empty
soundstage fronting impatient. Is potential of fearless.
Reputation carries a big stick and speaks anything but softly. Ill
conceived rests in hands of management. Hired gun wears a
black hat. Rides a black mount. Saves many a day.
Misperceived paints unearned headline. Splashes airwaves with
uncorroborated if not deliberate untruth though perhaps not
entirely unwelcome. Mick demands someone givin' shelter after
tearing down all walls, saved by hands later to be ravaged in a
face-save smear campaign.

Five Times To Mecca

Afraid of essence develops violent euphemistic, curable by neither academic nor mendicant, though exacerbated by the former, examining topographical maps in quest for notoriety unattainable via normal back channels typically greased through red tape yet the squeaky wheel ain't gettin' none. Crime scene cleaners rinse blemished pavement to something more agreeable. Call it floor-stripper toxic linguistic. Call it toxic. Turnstile coagulates with reprobate attribute scrawled in invisible ink under alphabet soup du jour. Five sided dice roll outside Cairo. I've never been though imagine ashtray and keychain sporting Cleopatra and King Tut and such kind bauble in spindly megamall of thatch commerce behind McDonald's. Facing Mecca to public address chants, bruising my knees. When in Egypt doing as the Romans. Ugly 'Merican. And proud or I think so anyway. Daggers pierce bulbous oculi. Another way of saying they're thinkin' something ain't kosher in my church which by chance happens to don torah rather than rosary- neither of which punches my ticket into cool submission. The checkerboard headdress seated a torso above a double hump grunts hateful. A cheap stab in the dark, the camel and tablecloth bit, but when working without light, one takes what one can mine assuming permit and mineral rights are intact. And word is chosen carefully. Better still, word chooses itself. In case of electrical or other type malfunction superseding drilled into skull oratorical resource, resort to description of what's in the safe. Not by name but etymology, content and purpose. Sketch an X marks the spot. I'll take it from there, reconstructing house of cards through cross eye. Very cross. Chasing lost pyramids in my sleep. Awaken to IED blast. Facing a water pale rippling an outline strangely resembling Mecca burning while ancestral homeland falls from the globe. Psychotic Persian plays American Woman. Gears and flaps operate and growl above as underwater hum delivers a care package with no return receipt to the unfamiliar with jukebox etiquette. A five slides into the melting plastic machine, I play Psycho Killer twenty times plus four bonus revolutions for the big spending. Drawing from halfway dead Johnny Red. Anybody for some nine-ball?

Angst

Uninvited burst of nervous attacks, squadron of your day ain't lookin' good strafe like. Tremors seize control of freezing branches pounding keys that seem to be punching their own beat. One the shakes can't find. Not a physical delusion. Rather unwelcome response to situation at hand and hormonal reminder of supremacy. Concrete casket about the soul. Convulsive freeze in tropical makes little sense atop alps. Legs twitch for warmth, giving peace to shivering hands until enunciated. The hands again quiver. A million wings circle the aviary. Their droppings, my art. Truism is a sticky companion. Stranded in an in need of repair fun house ain't much fun. Staring into a bank of counter angled, opposing and off center me, I catch a belly cramp. Looking to escape. Missing the coordinates to wherever. In desperate need of ginger-ale and bottle of Xanax.

Tossing A Line Or Two

Eternity goes on forever- quotes the same lines from old film. Walks the same streets, slinks the same alleys looking for prize in trash blaze ember. Report of gunfire stands first response at attention. Digital red flickers in time with siren blare. A shooting star dies of wounds received in ruthless reviews. Falls off a cliff after the wagon flips, depositing him on tired barstool. Knocks back slow death, swallows the worm. In an unappealing twist of fate, it's the worm doing the gnawing, leaving few crumbs for starling and finch. Interminable is a graph depicting distance between given up and no longer. Eternity or just another train depot depends on divine elixir of choice. Like the fly, cocktail napkins have short half-lives. Like heavenly tingle of crackling first hit. Never enough for ever again. Violated hymen gets last rights. I brush my teeth with paste that couldn't make a second truce with the tube. Another way of saying I'm swaggering repetitive, dealing cheap bromide. A warm shelter vain attempt at keeping sanity within reach no matter wrong direction taking the wheel. Goose is cooked though needs salt and a few quotables from yet to be viewed film, adding heat to the broth. Could all be merely replication repeating. Platitude is redundant though I believe that's common knowledge. Expanding horizon escorts smokestack back behind enemy lines. Ash catches red-eye jet stream home. Utopia is perfect. Perfect never is. Too impatient for boil, I grill cheese. And if unsuccessful, scribble superfluous bullshit.

Assault

A pockmarked landing strip continues to accept arrivals. Eden falls below sea level. Riptide justice enforces a verdict resulting in burial at sea. And the planes keep coming. And the grass blows in ubiquitous certitude, swaying to hurried trade-wind. A hundred tons of clouding up my fucking harbor drifts in. Monk finds resolution. And on his wings, sail- sail far. Gently rock in quilted sky, reaching for more which defeats the purpose. Settled on broken glass. Progressively heavier tonnage balanced precariously on a thorax sufficiently worn as to bleed sand. Sacred waters lap prime property. Natives toast coming of age. A bow to the dying. Aptly named locale honors all comers, living dying or otherwise. Too many flights clog the air and fields. I'm short on jazz. Long on the day. And deafened at the sight of disembarked, soon to make room for rainbow mutilation anew. Another floating Petri dish bounces offshore. Confirmation would be nice though bowel examination of two rocking monoliths doesn't follow scientific method and besides this more resembles some type seat of pants oceanography than rocket science. Nothing is up in the air but my seating on shoulders of whatever resonates. Careening off Carnegie walls in time though it's no signature with which I'm familiar. Perhaps acquaintance seeps below surface, unrecognizable until called into battle. After which, back to the drawing board erases grease pencil sketch. New plans are drawn striking in similarity to last. Briefly feels like a refreshing dip in a new stream. Up until I give it a good once over and a lady screams rape.

Zero

An address book never relinquishes ash. Journey of a thousand miles is bogged in landfill. Struggling with attempts to survive without anger is boiling the pot. Angst coats the crystal ball opaque although it could simply be drunk on too much to process. And it's all process, tempting aroma of island coffee and good smoke wants you to know. Fossil tumbles avenues as weed crossing Mojave. Present is marked absent. Tables turn counter clockwise. Search for balance throws equilibrium into a tail spin. Seesaw launches a kid to new heights when counterbalance apparition takes five. The blue parts in alleged deference to taffy and marshmallow though intent seems to hold less magnanimity. Kid hits playground with a thump. Scratch mark liberally adorns little black book with digital see ya. Shut doors to deception not self inflicted. Not without writing a fat check payable to the order of shut-in while allowing final search for elusive rabbit. And nothing breathing punched ozone ever will catch it but once. Search is yes and no, negating itself in mischievous but adhesive mathematical. End on the spot of the first breadcrumb- albeit sporting a substantially thinner set of matchbooks. Rage ebbs to my abject dismay. A primed bullet has but one mission. I'm still stuck on one plus its subpar twin. One process I know well. Can't say it's amiable, this particular relationship but shelling has waned. For the life of me, can't figure out here and now, just know the chimney sweep is long overdue. And I'm pissed.

Natural Beef

Organic beef is about to break out among wan vegan in the gluten free aisle. Fight for peace is oxymoronic- serves like ends as fighting for glory, remuneration or imposition of unwelcome ideal. Not ha ha funny that long hair peaceniks seem best at invective vulgarity, itself straddling grammatical lines. Insincere peace necks snap but that's just pleasant daydream. Hypocritical pens stop BP with oil base atop razed jungle. And the pine long for quick death, sobbing to the last. Emerald city who died and made you king resolves trans-fat and sugar are off the menu. Tobacco got cancer. Salt hides in the weeds, preparing for ambush which will arrive as anything but surprise. Steak is high on the agenda but the come-down is harsh. Butter's cooked. Land of free but for regulation established to create Stepford from Atlantic to Pacific and beyond. Vying for master race supremacy under cloak of impure consortium not bound by book of reasonable preamble. Millions die in a hot air chamber, attempting to comply with all new directives established when they themselves offered a finger only to discover missing limbs piled to Denver as logical conclusion. A no smoking sign adorns a tracheotomy type dive bar. Blaring warning just won't suffice. Morbid curiosity awaits patiently, fully aware that in short order short order will be banned and we'll all be drinking from the trough of can't get a little pregnant. Sopping gristle from blood plate with sodium enriched simple carbs, I ponder a square and fourth triple size caffeine delivery of the day. Not hurting a fucking soul though fucking souls have decapitated the serpent on my Gadsden flag. Something I can't abide in kowtowed silence. Labeled fascist, I point to Webster. Disheveled from perpetual non-consensual penetration and in what could be referred to as Freudian ironic, fascism got lost in the wrong section of the tome. Sandwiched between dogma and duplicity.

Skin Deep

"we are what we pretend to be, so we must be careful about what we pretend to be."

~kurt vonnegut, mother night

Examining a book by its cover. Wondering how much is cloak of darkness in black and grey. An unfired piece imploring distance for self protection. Tired of explaining presses vibrating needle across chaste naked skin. Underneath, a pirate's trove of skeletal remains. Dichotomous is master theme of mosaic. Unable to discover stimulating conversation is cue for trek of no destination other than relative peace of mind. Relative stinks like fish but it's all I can muster. Stone face ramble down boardwalk, civil only by grace of empty. Assaulted by a paper plate flapping in like ecstasy of vacant. Knowing too it's transient and life expectancy is determined by alacrity of spinning orange light approaching too fast for comfort. I could be ascribing too much knowledge to aimless refuse but then that seems the preferred method of current reasoning. And I hide behind my sullied hide. Dipping constellation spits chew on a throng of lurking in shadows before granting access to this type insanity. Asylum after light's out with roving degenerate and non compos mentis wandering hallway without borders. Loving persons hating people. Genetic mutation refusing to vacate. A misanthrope smiles internal regret at a beautiful child though slasher films play nonstop now that computer has replaced reel and accompanying intermission. Subservient geisha and irascible mamba guard my right. Phoenix does fly-by's over LA to the left. Bifurcated whimsy scattered about. All in place for eternal Halloween. A ledger too exhausted to open the books. The tome speaks volumes- renders me graciously mute. More so today than yesterday. Wine and roses. Quill and dueling pistol. Love and hate. Etched joy- a personal note, reminding of purpose. A tear drops from gravestone in live grass. I am conflicted. I'm man. Oiling my own entirety in allegorical collage.

Let It Bleed

(for my brother marko hartenbach)

Let it bleed. Let it be. Tap-dancing those two tone keys. Lingering in unbelievable paying no heed to the dial. Soaring two octaves past lucid for the lady. Taking 45 degrees at 90; 90 at 45. Breathing noxious dioxide, spewing magnificent oxygen. Crashing headlong into a thousand battling ruminations. Come out scathed though still punching. Spinning loom out of control reckless abandon yarn. Wings find purchase atop bent not broken. Present makes for momentary here and now. Shooting past with haste of a tweaking hare. Resembles reflux which tastes like last night. Damocles hang over is too much to stomach. Banging that drum and blowing that horn. Drunk on the nectar of essence. Seeking whole in pieces of a millennial puzzle. Floating with the jazz. Composing without conduction. Bossman now sings a siren's song. Visiting notes sail to East Liverpool. Stop on a dime. Home is where melody begins. Where it ends. Trumpets blare Appalachian blues. Madman across Ohio water, pied piper of the song. Letting it be. Just as she wants it. Completing the puzzle or at least a close enough facsimile thereof.

Whirling Dervish

Never a cog when you need one. Wheel spins something incessant. Spews lard on the bearings. Rolls on bouncing rumination pothole of eternal life. And the air is stagnant. An odor of burning flesh though only those in on the joke taste it. Genetic wrecking ball craters endoskeletal something vicious. Visible to no advanced medical apparatus. Cracked reflection jumps stagnant pond awaiting further instruction. Perhaps a roadmap hidden in quarry rock. Bats fly free. Guano permeates. Dawn is but another pop-quiz on what now. Judgment, a well too deep for audible splash yet shallow as a centerfold interview when taken out of context. Superego blasts what's left. There are few survivors. A thousand doves circle. Waiting. A lamp burns for eight days and nights on fume. A hamster concurrently burns the last of its wick. Whirl ebbs in whiteout crash- sires nascent spring. Doves chew their binds. And the bats...the bats mate furiously with emancipated lovebird. Conjoin codependent on a blank sheet traveling somewhere in the heart of genius. Genius of heart. And the wheel is but oxidized echo. Light as feather. Heavy as golden word awaiting renewal. Throwing sticks into malicious spokes. Walking hot coals to redemption. Proceeding unbridled momentum anew. And the road ends where it will end, tasting much like the blood of conflicted giant. Feet too large for otherwise ample creepers. Last spotted entering fire pit exit. Warpspeed. Trajectory vertical.

Shifting Moons

Penning a missive to no one. Flip a switch; light rapes sundown. Chills bones to brittle. Soul, blue. Cat eyes would assist. Cats die. Anonymous herd of exhausted migrate below. Their light prances gracefully in time. Disturbing not. It's close-ups I abhor. Let there be light. Somewhere else. Awash in somewhat blessed, hunger for peace or equivalent relative to warring idiosyncratic. Keeping temperature hypothermic. Only coffee, a modicum of hope maybe. And Coltrane blowing Alabama. Not a life, but with the latter, a charitable morsel of warm. Unexpected grin briefly passes over somewhere between here and nowhere. Hillbillies say it was retrograde's firm hold on mercury. Madmen stuck with voodoo hearts know otherwise.

Yogi Bear

Incendiary. Lightning upon drought laden woodland. Lit butt and gasoline. Carnage of medieval catapulted upon inside out. Ripping from the pages reading R.I.P. Jumping elated into a new realm of old rules. Codes written in blood of pubescent blossom neurosis. Shrinking no time soon. Sending mortar shells to distant rings around invisible moons. Message attached reads SOS. Responses are light years away. 911 just rolled box cars and a couple homies for good measure. Lost in undulating pit of swine and guts. Spinning mud tires on iced pavement. Dismembering an embankment. Tipping fortified something gettin' forty more. Hiding from illusory. Three-card Monte has an ace up its sleeve. Weather forecast indicates depression to continue. We have an app for that hates record players. Rotten hates everybody. Himself most, likely. A stairway to sentience ends in an eddy. Salmon talk. Leap faithfully in perpetuating pursuit. The noncompliant though smarter than average king leaps blindly into the mouth of something grizzly. Head-scratch why like. Slips through open hands which never definitively learn why but guess well. An avalanche came and passed. Twelve men on snow camels ate dinner. Then each other. Sometimes it really just is what it is.

Pink Cats

It's Floyd, the cacophony of notes colliding in orgasmic delight
and I'm drawn and quartered. Light is dim. Curtains hide me
from... Well, hide me. Warmer now. An opaque fir-ball
commonly considered bad luck watches my type. Enjoy
tempting fate, I do. Little one, though...still hasn't figured out
it's a binary rodent. Wish I never had. Big one couldn't care less.
Lucky bastard. And that little terror? 10" with a 5' vertical leap.
Claws of needles. Teeth, honed spikes. No regret but for after
the fact. What motherfucking havoc I would wreak were I to be
so blessed. Instead sitting here knocking nonsense. Hoping one
of the one people I typically share it with finds virtue within its
latencies. Stepping in front of the camera though not wanting to
be seen. Shine on you crazy diamond was written for someone
else. About that I couldn't care less. I'll just listen. Little cat's
still next to me. Angelic face demonic eye. Awaiting dark house
to begin festivities. Items crash in the night. Tired of getting up
to examine what died. Stoned. Needin' to get up and change
discs. Needin' to think about a meal. Wondering if maybe I
should hit the woods for a deer or perhaps tip a cow under the
light of the wind blessed skies. Of course hunting deer from a
sedan at dusk is generally frowned upon in these parts and not
so easy a task in So Cal anyway. Considering a number of
options for which I have zero interest and serve no good ends.
Meeting people like. You know- human interaction. Seems too
good to be true. Cost benefit analysis bargains pain and
suffering will ensue. Actuaries advise strongly against it.
Haven't often enough taken that piece of the rock with me in
interpersonal arena despite axiomatic omens. Someone certainly
will find more pros than cons by definition and all will smell like
roses after what's likely a quick jaunt through another dimension
with an entirely different being to please though you've yet to
please yourself however ephemeral is love. Under the scepter of
everything's fucked and nothing's ever gonna be better and
history hasn't shown the map a hundred thousand times and
what have you done for me lately as in time between
commercials on the we don't play music, just display short bus

gumbas in their natural habitat frequency...what fucking relationship of any variety can withstand all that? One in infinity liberally. I'll pay odds. You would too- assuming you allow yourself the virtue of honesty of self and statisticians. Yeah, but when in a casino... And the fucking world is a gambling hall. If you don't know that much by now, fuck off with Harry Potter. Or maybe you just find yourself in a rubber room with track marks, visible and otherwise besieging your vapid exoskeleton. Brought to bear by a series of negative interaction with traveling too near another's aura, bringing to light that which wasn't yet meant to be revealed. Nope. No clue either. Just going with the fingers. And thinkin' of spikes in arms. Think I'll put on the wall and dream opium dreams but some pretty decent, albeit far more tame animal will have to substitute in the final production. Stinky weed. Actually stoned. Think I said that before. Sorta proves it. Usually I just smoke it to keep from thinkin' I need to be any more comfortably numb than now. What the fuck is that kitten thinking?

Jump

Someone lit a candle. Several. And the luminescent riptide is pulling me under. Nervous energy is on reprieve, delivering confusion and an angst all its own. A drunkard, modicum of functional appearing kind, emerges from root cracks in pavement which refuse to yield. Malleable lives a long stretch. A virtue for which I've yet to gain much renown. No give holds or snaps. Similar to petrified dogma which sends the inebriate to irreparable street fissure. See it no differently today than yesterday. It's the figure brushing his teeth fronting the medicine cabinet I can't recognize. Disconcerting, this stranger in the house. However it's worth a confession: can't say I've ever been familiar with the report of the jigsaw glass though consistency regaled in a depression absent this day's lecture. The senior professor caught a nasty case of crabs from a precocious coed whose welcome papers mistook faculty for facilities when inviting her to make full use of the former, intending the latter I'm sure. The sub looks soft. Happy even. And this guy's teaching abnormal psych. Sorta makes sense where happy is non-sequitur in light of arithmetical progression preceding the smile. A rectangular bound oval best left to advanced statistics which after much differentiation, integration and tenured donut wars, conclude inconclusively nothing is abnormal to any degree greater than happy. Graveyard and cage and appliance box overflow with anguish riddled melancholy. Joyful are needles in casket stacks. Happy? Just doesn't follow. The soft sub drips his being on a fecund class in a tremendous gut dissertation deviating not an iota from his effervescence. Provides clear evidence that his sparkle is the human condition abnormal.   He noose-jumped from the hall's track-light. Neighbors and colleagues moan disbelief.   "But he was so happy." Tell it to the rope. And blow out those fucking candles. Something quick like. Wal-mart has a sale on loose Kevlar and the dog runs mad.

Chugging Along

Running on new grade of fuel. Not sure the timing belt has yet to cinch itself. It's seen the movie before. Broken promises of efficient lifeblood delivery with just enough undisclosed ancient Chinese secret to keep hunger pangs at bay. Soft rain darts across the window. Sweet honey keyboard nectar. Mournful tears of heaven born in furtherance of greater balance. There's a different hum in a tired engine. And song can't exist where silence is not. Hushed tone speaks from the pulpit- commands the grandest James Earl Jones deliverable outside the aforementioned's studio. In its dormancies lies truth of the matter. Grey matter. Scheming, plotting, planning, ruminating-order unimportant. Just a loop of wicked piercing lucidity. Psychiatrically impairments get it worst. Logical conclusion on scales of equilibrium would ergo imply the sane would then have it good. Of course the last infers sane exists. One could say it's in the eye of the beholder. And should the mass be so senseless as to adjudicate itself lucid simply by virtue of relativist comparison with those perhaps less in possession of faculties, then we're all rubber room ready. And Newton demands the universe must have another animate planet. A counterpoint to our infernal abyss. What a fucking bore. Nice place to visit. Like hospitals. I take my coffee black.

At It Again

Empty can be surrounded by yesterday's distorted vision of happy which never so resulted- simultaneously expecting a different outcome than that delivered during the previous experiment, which, parenthetically, was medically diagnosed as empty. The planet revolves. Always seems to stop where it started. And bounding about psychotic worker ant like, angels and demons battle for supremacy though it's clear and likely a topic of previous dissertation, one exists not with the other. What nature abhors fills like a swollen river, breaching levees in attempts to revert to the mean though discerning temperament is most transparent in what isn't said despite the repetitive nature of the verbose script.

Guzzled Deject

At a bar drinking angry. Determined destination- blitzed. Got there quick. Sunset laughed at me. Kirin to start, then Coors chased Johnny Red. Ripples far off are six foot chop surfing south. The trades pick up steam. Normally taken to amiable with barkeeps. Looked out for me, them. Kept me hydrated and such. Angry drunk night spoke only through gesture aimed at dead soldiers. Empathetic nods replied. All sound silenced by the din of Dead Kennedys' Biafra sneer singing of lynched landlords and chemical warfare. Four sheets in a one hour wind. Stood ready to battle alongside a walking mouth. Scratched DK adorned every school text I owned. Thousands others ended up in like receptacles in courtyards of another kind of box. Dream suck cask of sullied teen. That which bore responsibility for all DK's on all apathetic and dejected. His voice went old though shamelessly never allows for an open space. The call to arms, spurious at best. Laughably hypocritical could be more accurate. Thankfully the music and sentiment live on. And following the preceding superfluous regression, it bears note that the two fister on the stool was an adolescent in aging skin. Still drunk on old tunes. Still high from inane press to revolt despite utterly obscured objective. Ear buds piped in the chorus. I scrawled a couple commemorative letters on seven napkins. Paid the tab. Strolled up the road. Landed, literally, in Kalama Park, a mile or so. Rose and landed again. And again. Fell to my side and shared my drink with the sands. Called home. She knew. Grabbed me a few later. Jello and the gang never relented. There was a holiday in southeast Asia. And a minor disaster on a rock in the pacific. Who switched the reels?

Unsyncopated Yesterday

Remnants of the past are leaving a bitter taste. Time signature changing without prior notice and of no notice its own. Descending into a chasm recently ascended. Pressure builds. Typical of late would imply another bag going to the recycle bin. A heavy bag however, this. More readily punched than disposed. Split personality revealing additional crevices, previously undiscovered though not unsuspected. The mob has gathered at the meeting hall which never ceases to convene. Agreement never reached. Barring the door with transparent barrier is of no consequence. Deep breathing techniques continue to fail and Sikh daggers shoot decisive reflections lest one forget their piercing glare. Water under the bridge is a torrent. The span weakens. Condor and various of its ilk circle patiently. Soon, rotted flesh of dead relations will grace the collective beak. They probably won't like the flavor though don't typically quibble over such type trivia until digestion doesn't exactly clean the pipes. Descending further into the erstwhile unexplored and the popcorn trail is being consumed by whatever rodent species the gathering hall sit-in mob let join. Travelling by touch through the darkened corridors, chambers and the like. Rounding the corner, bumping into the entrance. Too many variables prevent deeper exploration though the text is obtuse enough as to allow for multiple interpretations or head scratches as the case is likely. Death stench permeates open space between world and protagonist. Not necessarily the bane as it would so appear. Occasionally instrumental tracks are more fulfilling than vocals. A drum beats something of no discernable pattern. Half a brick of straws, varying in length is delivered. Only two remain in the proverbial fist. Wagering sanity draws the short one. Though it's no closely held secret. In fact, odds are one to twenty. Five percent always bet underdogs though ninety five feel one among them. Separation anxiety falls to an all-time low. Distressed asset investors are feasting on the scraps though fools and their money never belonged together in the first place. Never underestimate the howl of seemingly minor squall. They invariably precede the freeze burn of a winter only Hollywood could imagine. Though with few exceptions are labeled 'based on a true story.' Few are uplifting or still-life recreations for that matter.

Up At Night

Circus performers in unflattering poses- rafter swinging-colliding mid-stream. A wine cellar guzzles fine bouquets which toss themselves into drunken shards as ennui reaches the highest of shelves. High is a working class hero never questioning contrast of existence, sleeping tight night. Low, brilliance stuck in its own glow, circumventing acres of happy for the sake of blessed, sinister insanity which is the prime mover of sleighs to depth of sugar and castor oil contradiction of that laying between first and last acts. Rich in this regard is anything but happy. Joy is purview of high- delineated above. Lost in the mix, a dopey lab chases its tail, never losing its smile and an ant brigade dutifully presses on in furtherance of ends not contrived which is a thin umbrella under which euphemism blossoms, sucking discourse its honesty in search of pool table level in a round hall where smoke violates clean air standards in an act of civil unrest gathering in the beams above. Knowing consequence, I light a red. Inanity sleeps foot to head with Nietzsche. Order from chaos or perhaps just making the best of untenable circumstance. Perhaps out of control though never blind to the fact. Despite previous suggestion, the circle is off center, never quite finding connection with the beginnings though comes asymptotically close. And a battalion of retaliate rises from the wreckage of an errant meteor shattering hope for a linear solution to a dynamic of physics of gravity and consequence. Absurd is an unfortunate mia in current linguistic preference. This perhaps due to a fear of mirrors. And something greater than a minor case of acrophobia, not to be confused with a clear and ubiquitous case of agoraphobia among many straddling borders of missing synaptic links. The funambulist pose after aforementioned multiple collisions is equally unflattering as a naked corpse splattered atop prop and red nose type. Intestines splayed, cranial cavity never recovered. Or perhaps just jarred by too many concussive blows, contents crash the falls of neurological wastewater pouring through the not insignificant crack in a tortured psyche. I hate clowns. Another recurring theme. Like greed for more fine wine to dull the senses to whatever's at hand. The hand is infected and likely to be excised. If only woeful undeparted grease of hostile wheels was so yielding. If only the impressionist needn't fear a clear lens. Insane are rarely bored in the wheelhouse, but with an industrial drill like intangible, continuously bored as a rifle until the soul is released forevermore through a gaping hole which calls into question in whose image is creation. I don't sleep tight.

Hittin' The Skins

Written out but fingers persist. Fill blank with artificial letters atop a thunderstorm canvas courtesy of the deadly fruit. Lightning fires bolts en masse- leaves the best of archers dazzled. Electric rays shoot between cumulous gatherings of forceful anger raining above. Fury unleashes brilliant destruction of artificial construction. Distant vision notes vast expanse separating the arrows. Each appears more menacing by virtue of its split from the others. Earthly fractionalization creating its own art. And at the risk of anthropomorphizing the inanimate, it seems the atmosphere is fully cognizant of the grandiose statement it makes in its revolutions. As if it's seen all painted. Read all texts. Invaded the mind of Pollock. Watched as the lone apple fell atop physics, changing our complexion for eternity. And if this living breathing spec on the intergalactic map does in fact understand in some ethereal kinda way, they found it on a stage. Beating the beat with Copeland and Cameron and a reverberating apparition pounding skins precise and hard- R.I.P. John. Alabaster lesson in what lies concealed in a void so mindfuckingly perfect. And with speed and certainty of a hundred cruise missiles, the empty air is filled with the guts of genius, standing in for silent. Like the disparate lightning bolts, appearing to be catching the same minimal point.

Decay

In this town, streets sparkle. T-bone alleys provide cover for nefarious and shelter for indigent. Putrid air represents with a urine base. Composition of tertiary odor is something best not thought of. Raindrops rinse street walk lycra of congregated bodily fluid. In this town, streets freeze in the dead of summer. Hiding space is bombarded with nouveau lounge reject and bass heavy din. Violating whatever is questionably referred to as civil in this jungle, my town- that which kills small children at low volume, sails from behind the quaking velvet to the heart of holy land at eleven, one louder. Butts litter the rain glisten underfoot in a circular pattern cut from the dimensions of a lone canopy, fifty feet from the door as required by rule of law. Law is the mechanism by which men control man. Control is a funnel of preferred habit channeled to the desired holding pool. And this water never shines. Post coital latex deposits surround parking spaces not well lit. In this town, this grand experiment forever in flux and the parks teem with unnoticed avian and reptile. A sign is missing four of its limbs in a tribute to economy. Faded into history as the bodies who line her streets. The youngsters wake to the night and infiltrate suspect humanity as only youthful hubris commits. On liberating rooftop or encased in lightly traversed stairwell. In barely clean enough motel rooms and efficiency units in dilapidated nods to past glory. Nobody cleans the pigeon shit off faces anymore though the pavement is pressure washed, temporarily uprooting that already without purchase.

Doesn't Follow Or Does It

(for doug knott)

Was suggested the parts functioned well, though the whole was something less than the sum thereof. That somehow indications of failed gravity juxtaposed against a sculpture of the Madonna may present something of an interesting cerebral cluster fuck however never imbibe on linear cohesion. A Roman fiddle heard as a Greek tragedy befalls another as greasy hands slip a boulder down the hill where it falls atop a sword killing both he who would want for high places and the ruler granting his wish, the whole while it's the Ottoman burning and a cross is deconstructed under the weight of its disciples and supernova careen into one another and Ferraris fall from cliffs and while following a good midget buggering, clowns all thankfully die and collagen explodes all over reality TV. A city grows and shrinks concurrently under the watchful dilated caricature that's trippin' hallucinogen like as thugs hide indiscretion from soul-pimping smartphones and federal choppers drop microphones into corked bats atop the masses, cars spew blood, smokers' cough wheezes and carnal knowledge is declared illegal sport. Statutes relating to reform of pork barrel spending are held over a barbeque of multi-cultural baby backs and the servants we've all become in acceptance of the absurd fate of the absurd galaxy or out of virtue misdirected to an alternate cosmos by an evil genie with an angelic face. And planet reason, though there isn't any, is in the rearview of the camel as its cancer dances in the sunset window far from said globe- and all this is apparently a series of plot deficient non-sequiturs. Seriously?

Out Of Tune

Familiar winds blow like superfluous notes injected into harmony which never quite materializes under the might of extraneous. Cars flatten cats of manifestly too little curiosity. Expectation demolishes those of too much. Overanxious trumpets blow, then silence in sound-proof rooms whose key is held elsewhere however is too sharp even for serpent tongue. All of which croons volumes though from which text I'm reading, I remain unsure. Locked in a bedroom of ostensible comfort. Attempting to see the minors fall into organic line before known quantities wield a saber before me and cry dry tears marching in the shadow of my dirge. Dancing to my sodden bones. Offering maudlin worthless. Still tripping on or over my ethereal word rather than my song which is incomplete and off key at that.

Steppenwolf

Hopeless awakes hopeless. Wrought with pain none can see. War with the inner being while outside, the world impales soul like no dagger might. Mundane engulfs surroundings. Neither warm nor cool, even. Mornings are grieving now and later. Recurring agony not of a gracious enough disposition to end the madness and throbbing, invisible to all but by virtue of actions and tenor. Most can't read...late-night strolls through wherever...lone wolf...mis-self-diagnosed as man of two voices even as din of hundreds plow through him hot knife through skin like. Faces are blank putty bustling to get to one place or another to maintain nothing more than even keel. Agoraphobic. There is no hope, only survival on a flat plane on a round continent. Trying to come to grips with this and the beast within. Ludicrous contending with a lunatic planet. No great purpose but word. Society viewed through a prism casting dichotomy inward to the lone wolf battling the human. Fails the final test. And then she was gone. Alien planet. Ferocious at once kind. Prowling at night. Awaiting the next catastrophe to befall before the magic. And the voices got their voice. All possibilities elastic yet the theater goes dark. Then she was dead.

Battery Park To The 34th

"the night was full of nazis"
~s.a. griffin

The Tennessee night was full of rambunctious Nazis. Swastika stars eclipsed a sky already opaque behind smoke from clean burnt scalps which permeate the atmosphere- disrupt rhythm- trailer park to poisoned sea. An unsympathetic crowd grew restless. Ensued a giant melee. Hasn't happened here for hundred fifty years kinda brawl. Brown shirts, white caps and skin-heads head north. Seek fertile ground for their Doc imprint though little soil was fertile and the good doctor rolled over in a steel toed grave. In the emerald city of crossbreed, the white Reich started low, greeted with falling bodies of technology- replaced employees on the street. They attempt an assault on Switzerland for their neutrality. Try firebombs on their finances though someone forgot the lighter. Goldman grabbed his sack and dumped a million quarters atop their numbers. Seeking shelter in Chinktown, flaming fish heads were delivered at high- speed from ancient though clearly functional catapults. The remaining Reich ran north, marched up third; many die under a hail of spike roast from Jewbucks. Roaming further north, quietly ignored by those who provide the lynch mob funding from behind closed newsroom doors in a project codenamed Rosebud. Interestingly, St Patrick's was awash in a reassuring fountain of pristine water. Off East, running into scarlet letter Hassids peddling their rocks, brandishing white hot brands of their own. Passing Roc Center, Atlas shrugged and a globe fell upon them. Back to northside, spear-chucked from Harlem. Buried in unintelligible Spanish or something like it but missing odd three or four nouns and verbs in a single phrase up near the Dominican 34th. Numbers are dwindling. On their tail, Spic Kike Nigger Nip Chink Wop Towel Head Pot Head Mixbreed Halfbreed, even a few Kraut and dozen mongrel dog NYPD. All due haste, those left run for a beacon. Lone Southern Methodist church. All eviscerated upon arrival. The ash falling upon ember piles in crop circles somewhere south where urban Dixie lives strong and banjos own a bayou. Crucifixes shoot misappropriated symbols from the sky. Navaho cheer. Christ falls from his. A briar head piece is remarking less pointedly. He goes to synagogue the first time in 2012 years. Surgeons patch his wounds. He heals theirs. And arms himself with an assault rifle. Bloomberg, Napoleonic dictator mayor at hand, drops dead. Not much more than a banal sidebar serving none but the author though that is his purview. Digressing, some albatross don white Stetsons as they shit atop your head if, of course, you're looking up. Somehow they know. Finally the man of any color, the destitute and downtrodden see himself in his eyes. The hopeless find hope. A skywritten note appears though no plane is visible and the cursive cloud doesn't dissipate. One reintroduces itself to one. The night was full, yes so full. Of Nazi blood. Awoken by feet that no longer stank, an Atheist Jew smiles.

Hell In Heaven Or Invert

(for s.a.)

Archaic translations of current events tangle the web in which they're entangled. Woven yarn repeatedly re-stitched unravels at key plugs of the needlepoint. Kindling sapling readying an all out inferno outline replaces the bucolic. Still she stitches. Spiked horns aim for the heart of the decayed artichoke which stands in for apple orchards. Lost in translation is an unyielding outline provided. Guttural chorus emanates seeking firm footing on a shaky podium though steadfast in the wobble. Invading shores of intangible though never quite hitting beach sand. Preordained outcome releases subconscious its liability. Denies its majesty. Suffer sane does the head to the grindstone. Ache silent and rage conspire incessant in futile try for a burial without breath. No time to waste and abject fear bear a bastard child- genetics incapable of reality staring him in the cracked actor swallowing self in the name of barely concealable false pride and Hollywood swagger ball-gag torture. Sun reigns the parade. Floats explode. Throw far and wide black roses disinterested in repetitive nightmare certain to follow. Attempt for comprehension is blocked at the gate. Instructions on the door-sign are etched in crumbling shale. Overdue notes in dry hydration pouches bring nothing intoxicating but seem to complete the unintelligible puzzle whose answers lie in a paint by the numbers drawing unable to oblige silence of pencils not flying free in deference to missing tiles in a prehistoric maze of inscription whose revised edition seems spurious at best. The tapestry ends up needling the yarn to submission. A boy shivers in a dark alley somewhere else.

Art Of Marko

(for my brother marko hartenbach)

An ugly portrayal of a sacred heart beats through the veins of he portrayed. A genuine halo hovers above. Breathing arrested by excessive weight and none whatsoever. Dissonance reigns in the library which more than occasionally blows at the seams. Pages fly uninhibited only to reconnect through mediation conducted by artistic genius in the brilliance shelves never considering the arbitrator was the explosive. Chuckles rise from mathematics that only seem to indicate a lack of humor among statistical types that fail to see the square for its circle. Dewey is flippin out, running out of points. A boy sits between a war for which purity wasn't intended. The sacred heart beats through poorly tied sutures though somehow blooms in the art of a child never allowed whimsy when whimsy counted. Paying the price today for the veiled blood he rains upon the humble masses. Something the math section can't explain though perhaps Einstein might have. Lover not keen on that story and fighter (ditto) finds himself beneath a mountain. Climbs out to another nadir providing for another climb. The process is a never ending quest over crests into the valleys of creation. Painted with a toddler's stroke of sage brush, quietly showering essence of the epoch through a secret code one must earn if to fully savor the lyric. A dearth of options accompanies a trove of glimmering hope. A man sails above. Beyond. And perseveres even as the voices scream in terror and the echoes are deafening.

Bound

Malted milk burning holes through stomach lining- creates no friends in the process. Genuflecting weak grow ever more weary by the shot. Lost in perpetual confusion is a head pickled in bottle of no mercy. Mercy falls under a speeding bus- collapses when confronted. Disingenuous prosaicism is a laboriously constructed molehill crushed in the time it takes to pass superseding legislation to that which usurped the previous following a fifty thousand blank page Supreme Court dissertation on predicate case law. Digging for reason where logic is hogtied in resolute though unclear ransom note leaves hostage and taker in a heap of opaque, leading to an illogical solution that makes no sense. Sense is beauty in the eye of the sentient. A granite wall to dense brilliant. Anonymous hole in an untended field of forgotten to the simply lost. A chasm inching wider by the pint. Warning lights are airplanes piling in gutters blaring someone took a wrong turn somewhere. The royal someone, royal somewhere. Nothing ties it all together but for the common shoe in need of new laces. Stretched thin and snapping to inattention with alacrity of retirement home orgy. Something less shocking than a redundant front page suffering historical nonsense as redundant as the author's literary representations. Enduring is a multi plane mural on shrooms. Spiral staircase undulating, respiring underfoot. The banister ends in deceptive fashion- infinity pool illusion like. None-too-cautious hare slips. Lands in a thump. Thumper was shot and skewered on a spit. Tasted like chicken is cheap cliché but finger licking true. Bambi's ol' man adorns a mantle in Northwest Pennsylvania. Effigy of all under a flag embellishes a geometrically offensive office on northwest Pennsylvania- high on premium grade pruno brewed in a silo deep in the dust belt. Distributed by innocuous looking conveyances of horrific. Painted in supple texture. Driven by faceless perpetrators lacking discernable features to assist a line-up. Peering while not weaving between lanes will result in criminal prosecution and forfeiture of additional benefits. Mandatory minimum is a slot fronting convenience stores with a paper cup and ID badge reading: Veteran's Affairs. Stomach lining optional. Reek of ferment not prerequisite but preferable to that of Capitol Hill and may return a reduced sentence by local authorities of ostensibly more humane tendency and ownership interest in distant untended fields. Taps plays though all flags have been lowered half staff so often that the distance between banner and pole has been rounded by asymptotic cry of uncle, to zero, negating any need for further formalities.

Sweating Fray

Awoken to a day that eats itself as most others. Pumping iron
though I've yet to leave bed. A horse drawn carriage inverts and
wheels a low quality portrait of the horse. Under ever Gook is
an American waiting in line to be a Gook or anything on another
side of any pond though no restoration is to be found when the
virus has gone global. An empire melts under neon letters
forming Samsung in the sky. Under every citizen, some ex-pat.
But for the red lineage painting deserts a magical rust patina on
proud creased faces. Resentment isn't found in the hill and
cactus mesa of shameful genesis though spiritual salvation. Not
in the dead, buried or those yet interred. Hate is the domain of
the zombie. Neither here nor there unless conflict presents its
inveterate repugnancy. Awaiting venal secretion wherever it
may be found. Hiding in your nearsight. Traipsing headlines
for fresh flesh, buttery and sweet. Coagulating under the
heavens. Seeping into essence via pores too battle weary to close
ranks. Destroying hope with forged steel of mystical anvils
which never spark until after the strikes have ceased and the
sword has been returned to its megaphone scabbard fashioned
in the shape of division. Where no war exists, war exists.
Bubbling over in wicked ecstasy wherever two people shall
meet. Where those within earshot of an unfriendly neighbor
take offensive action in attempts to silence their own demons.
And the world's most prodigious murderers govern under the
who else we got principle. Seceding is no longer laughing stock.
Stock in trade is punishment at all costs. Costs are prices paid
without deference to consequence. Continental battle flags are
produced febrile in pace. A sentry stands guard awaiting
insurrection. The iron I'm pumping is lead- toxic passing via
osmosis or maybe diffusion- I forget. Thankfully the day
swallows the last of its diseased syphilitic jism allowing for
breath before eastern light rises in the collective cock that is
America. That is humanity. Depraved is homogeny constructed
of force. A universal pressure cooker bellowing for a tall cool
one. Receiving a hotter flame for its troubles. Seems the day

ain't totally digested yet.   Tomorrow's typeset speaks of exploding cookware.

Splintering Marble

Unattached universal ideal separates from dogmatic. Pulpits burn. Pious is elsewhere. An innocuous enough appearance caught on honed coat-hook in cathedral celebrating eternal life which skins definition to the bone. Bone dry sacramental chalice accompanies crumbs in a bowl. Flock is shorn. Face follows tail blind. Edificial deficiency buries the gist of things with flamed trident. Atop a bed kneel the righteous. Somewhere beneath heaven a hundred suits, two hundred chapeaus seek new digs. Scramble over cliffs as would tend to follow when trailing sightless where no jeweled arch collects alms. Next to a kitchen, faith rises in steam of tv dinner. Well vested slaughter a lamb in deliberate cannibalism. First born males drown in holy water of a sea that never parted but in lore as is written and rewritten following multiple edits of previous rewrites. No deliverance follows. Bushes burning are not political but presage eons of holocaust. One under god in self affirmation repeated excessive. Overtly superfluous cannot be given much credence. Somewhere in a garden blossoms bloom and leaves of grass bend to the sun, rising to the occasion when not stunted. Cat call of blasphemous cuts through curtsy on a rug through sets of superior amplification, drowning out tribal ritual. Yarmulkes slip from heads. Confessional unveiling offers redemption from deliberate blind with signature stamps for transfer papers. Endeavor to obscure bread crumbs to responsible. Pissing contest results as judged by Olympus throw gold about Athens. An Unitarian plane circles before a southern something or other blasts it from forever. And next to a summer lake, faith is youth embracing original passion in a mossy bed smelling of something bigger. Honeyed. And maybe a flask of Jack. Delivered by ours is not to question why. Shelter from hellfire despite no adequate top cover nor ceremonial rite. Only initiation to carnal love innocent as shooting star. Radiance likely to wilt in the passing of suns as such is the price of admission. Ordained by whatever name who lives not in any house but a corner of heart, assuming a complete cavity. Assumption is poison in a caplet yet to emit its narcotic.

Sacrificial Slams

Unhealthy doses of reality are irradiating fingers-crossed hopeful sentiment. Altercation replaces...nothing actually. History presages history. Carrion and other form of detritus rot further into man's inhumanity to all under any sun. Yoga type conjecture pulled its head out of the mat, bearing a frown-suffers vagary like the rest. A path through a thicket two miles from wherever it is you're lost. Your GPS refuses to recognize the G. Have a cow man. Even bovine intellect chews anything in its field of operation. Grenades jump from empty foxhole close to the erstwhile granola contortionist kind. Drawing scimitar imported from black empire of Italian tablecloth hierarchy. Catches head in Tibetan cloud off guard. Battling eastern mystics of peace are joined by Sikhs, whoever the fuck *they* are (seriously, I can't be alone here). Knowing not for which hemisphere to shed dagger blood. Not flying high is still up in the air. Grounded sparks to life- grinds to a temporary respite nearby. Hard to recognize, grizzled and worn though upright. Limping into today. For now. Calendar unscheduled. Aren't they all? Racking the bean for another means of expressing something or other is futile - exercised muscle like. Not good kind sore next day. Or is it following? Days are streams running together seeking a greater tributary. Nothing is nowhere. Where the doves fly is laden with buckshot. Rudolph's red nose has been chafing the wrong trough and he endures a thrashing and reevaluation of sympathy liberally sprinkled on his legend. Elves are NBA stars chopped off at the knees. Sacrificial lambs served with mint jelly provided by the players' union. Rusty cages bang to the tune of metal clanking oxidized. Cardboard card houses blow in trailer park whirlwind. Another cheap jab at sad but true. Santa's a lesbian construction worker in the off season. Subscribes to European grooming standards. Never seen one smile so much- lesbian construction worker. Maybe it's Lebanese reconstruction worker I had accidentally Googled earlier. Though they can't be smiling much either I dare guess. Landing skid busted on the sleigh. Technology replacing labor in northern freeze catches a doozy of highly contagious sniffles. Doctors remain guarded against nurse suits with a gilded adornment here or there. Need more lambs. Jazz labors the scale- collapses guard rails during an improvised regatta turned deadly as prevailing wind section flipped to doo wop which never appeared happy with the transition. And under all this, quicksand. Debt clock runs twenty four hours but apparently is about to throw a talk to the hand after a no-pay decision was rendered by officials requesting anonymity. Buried in the miasma, a youngster digs himself out. Rapidly returns to the warming vituperation he knows however is careful to rub a rabbit's foot forty days in case monsoon season has been slated to take longer to complete than forecast. Holds a heavy book of ancient parchment with free hand. Beef ribs in the smoker.

Cold Forge

Hammer and sickle explodes rubles in a sucking vortex of learning from the best. Under the table bangs its head on full disclosure. Full is a fluttering flag unsure of its virtue. Chaste, an antiquated notion of moral absolute under wavering stars. In eyeshot of partially blindfolded and measured nearsight of French construction. Rats leave her garden due to an unexpected lotus chill. Brown leaves hit muddy grass before radiating in shifting hue of autumnal. Wasted potential stepped upon as if nonexistent. Less than affable build a pipeline transmitting ill gotten into bottomless wells. Blue pinstripe replaces flat grey. Siberian wolves howl jubilant battle call. American freedom fighters are busy elsewhere. Foreign enemy hides that within. Disarming foul cries are obfuscated by din of divisive. Se habla Russian. Questioning faces peer lip licking lascivious in a one eighty discussion with evil empire on recipe for battle plans laid for conscription devices. Perhaps additional white noise to divert attention from a trillion smoke and mirrors gone up in smoke though the good kind is still sin as divined after a couple wood shop instructor like two finger pours of Kentucky. Pizza delivery statistics reveal nobody cares but the back slap crowd of I'm not a drug addict, spill me another. Red scourge receives instruction on superfluous confinement from land of the free as a party favor. Stalin and pilgrims argue over who ended more dreams in creation of opposing pyramid schemes. Popular domestic opinion plugs its ears. Throws in a few la-la-la's for insurance purposes. Hallmark says it all for a price. Self design was greenlit ages ago. An endangered species though related regulation is purposefully ignored to great effect if declining number is any indication. Symbol of oppression is replaced by two hundred year old design of some old lady who may have simply been knitting to kill time in anticipation of Hansel and Gretel. Running into ideal of vacillating laid in stone by accident. Cheeseblocks fall on weakened necks. Aisles full. Wallets shrink. A dichotomy difficult to dissect within unending bowl of new Kool-Aide. Rockets' red glare illuminates novel analysis. New year resolves to improve however says same thing annually. Repeated at various points throughout revolutions about a repulsed sun, seemingly intent on hiding its glow from sea to soiled sea. Over hill over dale, over gravestone conspicuous in no inscription. Over gladiator pit of institutional. A bed of ten written in stone is jack hammered to submission. Red and blue refuse to make purple. Universal bruise excepted.

Stitched Throw-Aways

Restless bats are laying waste to my morning cortex- dive bombing into synaptic what the fuck. Mood appropriate music is tripping through the dark chords. By chance it's not appropriate. Slamming into concrete wall in syncopation with the rodent birds in the attic. They ain't toys. A Pandora's box never violated when searching beam plywood and asbestos for trivia. Cracked open by the evening flyers. Mashed into a god if you just get me out of this, fingers crossed behind back promise to be broken. Wrapping into a nonsensical cloud of vapid interior. Just an outline yet to be found by the magic marker. Sketch likely won't be satirical. Orchestral comedy section has flown the coop. Leaving just its counterweight. Seasick takes on role of balancing act though never took lessons. An empty theater. Perhaps a lonely keyboard, scratch pad of tears and fears. Far off a star casts a temporary climate change though I always question intention. Paranoia looms large in unbalanced. In shadow and castle, exhausted rodeo clowns miss the hole in the barrel. Get impaled. Cloak of invisibility drops- leaves not so much as a fig leaf. In a schoolyard, puberty sits naked before its peers. Not a flannel to conceal heart's skeleton skipping beats to a different drummer. Pounding so hard and never missing the worn spot on the skin. No textbook hides burgeoning lumber as the unattainable passes, pom-pom in hand. Mocking reproach barks in the key of laughter. The most perfect repudiation. He awakens in a self conscious jolt. Soon thereafter, laughter is taken from the soundtrack. Cackling steps in. Distinction of deceptively wide schism. Some might respond with a parallel argument. Clearly never introduced to the latter. Satire of hooting understudy ain't nothing but inhuman. Though wines bloom so too does vocabulary become pliable. In quest for ADHD common denominator, it's likely the 'in' has been stricken and it's unfortunately all too human. Cynical is always a safe bet. It's Christmas. Somewhere Mencken regales with the hyena. Hit to the ten ring sort of scornful. Audience members unfortunate enough to giggle are summarily executed.

There ain't enough rope for the throng of it'll all be well if i just laugh.

Unpunctuated Queries

"i'd rather know some of the questions than all of the answers."
~james thurber

Overflowing cascade in interminable search for explanation. Deeper understanding is a blockade of senses. Erstwhile philistine is cutting blood supply to left hemisphere. Unleashed angel blows trumpets towards circle in square dichotomy- tips halo to an uncoreographed ballet flying unrestrained under stars shooting their mouths off- kneels before creative imperfection. Bowtie Chablis croquet match pits Ivy League can't tie shoe unassisted kind against a crew of whatever rags we can put together. The latter laying mallet to the former. Sucking down a frosty pint of Boston's favored son after. Washington drinks mouthwash by the case yet can't get rid of sticky truth pulling layers off the palate. Who's not rolling over in graves is a shorter list. Serpentine tracks in arid sand lead back to the same numb patch of smoldering. Enemy at the gate no longer presents as a Trojan horse though it's likely a red herring among a multitude additional puzzle. Losing a tale in cyberspace looses silent scream ISP to ISP. Googled googol only to find no truth in advertising and they're yet to come close to that many hits. Could explain surreptitious letter-smithing. Confrontational gestures are consciously mistaken for welcoming, indicating exactly how unconscious all is. Earth tones keeping the asylum calm. Expectations for something above smacked to lucidity. Seems ground covered previously. Abjectly absurd takes many a page in the book penned. Especially so if that inked is to be given weight. Taking the bellow to a faux fireplace is less vain than might seem. Shuffling repetitious is cornerstone to all farm animals in the great game reserve. Living, breathing its own without need for rancor of hard steps on the dwindling surface. Not so lucky is that touched by two legged devils smiling in knowledge Sunday will relieve them their transgression. A white dove sits on my sill. Actually a weathered grey cousin with poorer reputation. Willing to scrape where kindred lay droppings. Ergo the embellishment, though can't blame a guy for trying. Feeling the maligned comes easier. Alabaster implies purity implies perfection. Something entirely unfathomable. Flat and so utterly devoid of virtue. Exiting hibernation, another straight line ensnared by slinky logic signs on the dotted line. Dissenters succumb to their own free-will. Or lack thereof.

Atheist Christmas

It's the day before. The eve. Magenta paints a misleading argument outside. World falling asleep rejoices the birth of co-opted lessons never learned or at least a stocking stuffer or two. Hammer to nail equals a house of crystal, exquisite carving, pious mural of impeccable creation and a healthy stash of gold inconspicuously sealed within pestle and mortar. Reading backwards perhaps, though nothing remains in Hebrew. An imposing gate fronts the doors gilded in nudge and wink faith. Trapped inside, incredulous effigies of guaranteed absolution mistaken as representations of a savior by easily confused or perhaps just a lazy congregation with nothing but to shrug perplexed. Gathering steam once per week. On the day of rest. Non-sequitur, a device which inevitably loses punch behind its purposeful unveiling. Non-believer typing notes of faith by the nascent moon may seem like a candidate too. On the day of rest boggles senses to the sidelines for neurological review. And on the seventh day, he rested. Isn't that the gist? An unsympathetic exaltation arrives from every corner as intended target hits snooze. Whispers 'they're unworthy anyway,' drifting back to sleep. Another planet genuflects on Wednesdays. Some Tuesdays. Giving time to recover from the nap. Begs forgiveness lives in hearts true 24/7. Distended belly of profiteering keeps later hours, refusing to see the disapproving exhausted nod between arms held in a bloody t-formation. Spigot runs full throttle, risking timing belt issues. Metaphor mistaken for gospel is invariably an octave high. Maybe it doesn't follow that a devout Atheist ruminates over matters of the cross though it stands that perhaps within un-genuflecting rest best questions which may result in unwanted collisions at intersections of faith and organization. Then again some without fast rope escape route tend to find tasty morsels within the translated text. Transcendent allegory defying compartmentalization into subset of science nor human behavior though the latter doesn't live a hefty cab fare from whatever cable news catastrophe plagues a planet seemingly all too prepared to plague itself, regardless of faith or lack thereof which in itself is simply faith by another name. On island or alpine apex. A dark street of a lonely sojourn, someone spills my name in prayer to something beyond reach and to which I'm apparently often unkind. Of course, I'd reply with something akin to 'institutionalized bound faith ain't nothing but an easy way out.' Intention dominates convention in a best of seven MMA bout. Unfortunately I wouldn't know the easy way out if a map hit me in the head anyway. Piety lives strong though often tenuous in implementation. A rolling landscape of peak and trough in which the secret is buried. Hinting at the answer would be to say whatever spirit might inhabit soul, it's in the shoe of the believer as he trudges through existence like an uncooperative aging flea with broken back refusing to open up. Nowhere within marble arches is anything worth more than pecuniary. It is in a small town in Ohio. A forgotten hood of Los Angeles still recovering from divine fury fifty years hence. And always in deepest corners of our everything where pay to pray collapses under self serving dogma and top secret security clearance required to review records. Literary education, great debate back to BC. Evolving storyline punches out for the day. Waiting for a box bearing its name under a tree slaughtered for the sake of appeasing the one who apparently sired it. Now there's something that follows. On the other hand, up high, so well adorned claim rights to an ethereal sentiment from where great benevolence is stated platform of questionable integrity though outside granite walls finds legitimate purchase. In little girl's time of needing a puppy to replace the terminated companion she once loved. In the heart of small boy needing a liver though always of a pleasant disposition. Yet some pray for me. Whenever and wherever it seems to be needed. Emotion well received. Knowing not all the answers is virtue. Accepting highest of one's values isn't giving in for remuneration but allowing for affirmation within the prayer, implication of something worthy in a questioning set of boots rarely sure of their imprint. Whole of which is painfully absent the class of can't believe. Especially those yet to come to grips with themselves, grateful for the blessings befallen them from whichever source.

Nothing

Something's pulling at me. Actually the something is nothing which would seem to explicitly evoke an interpretive dance around whether nothing is therefore something. Greater minds have imploded under lesser weight. Skating on thin ice with inner beast though his teeth aren't so sharp. He's tired of the war of no name nor physical manifestation to the untrained. Falling from a cliff is a hard wake up. Picking up steam as hours pass. Squinting through the blue, promise of nightfall loosens day-lit disquiet. An anaconda unravels before crushing his prey. Measures of no progression with which I'm familiar have walking on thin ice sensation. Disruptive tendencies assault burgeoning there just might be something at the end of the tunnel worth sticking around for. Trippin' me up wherever possible. Floating on every note piercing the smokin' microphone yet fail to lift high enough to avoid low flying aircraft. Somehow it all comes off as nothing. Yet I'm doing something. Nothing. And we're back where we started. Right? A Turkish tapestry sports some interesting weaves or perhaps just coincidental that appearing is baseball split in half. Apple pie burnt to a crisp. Mother exposed for what she really is. Still nothing keeping me up at night though keep a jaundice eye on the Persian looking Turk rug salesman. More nothing. Lost within the something. Which is nothing I can figure out. Maybe that's what's got me feeling pulled. The great void bringing me closer to me. Farther and farther from them, including the she's. The beast is beat. Tapping a rarely unwelcome solitary rhythm, too worn out to smell the flowers in pots all around. More nothing. Or maybe just an excuse for understandable lack of inertia on anything related to relationship. That's something kind of. And it's a something I want nothing to entomb myself within if I do in fact have nothing spelled out right.

Ornette

Intoxicating yesteryear is a step to slower times. A shimmy to heights thought inaccessible yet devoid of pinnacle fear. Cresting up up and away. Dragging no longer kicking and screaming to harmonics bursting through smoky red brick. Bounding careless into the night. Missing a note which is left for dead though, springing then off another missed which together makes head spin in heart's delight. Let's split to New Orleans we're implored. A dirty dive in the old village or high-rise big buck shin-dig. A lonely stretch of central which once bustled free for the chained colored water-fountain crowd. Sitting in the shadows. Entering some otherworldly time-warp. Wondering what happened in the interim though not dwelling on old calendars dating things to come. Just suckin' in the vibe, dig? Touch of whimsy allows flight untethered. Pointing to that time-warp again. Where 20-20 hindsight longs to see before it. Imbibe within it. Or maybe, just maybe, it's nothing but an anachronism never to be heard again. Reminding that the jazz is alive and well in an eerie accompaniment in the cracks beneath our feet. The cars sputtering along with wide eyes. Homeless insane who have all the tip tap in their drunken gait yet remain blind to what it is. In the trees carved with initials and hearts beating together for now. In graffiti implying not so pleasant outcome. In the girl walking streets on a tightrope. Old buildings refusing to yield. Parks springing to life as the children running gratefully amok upon sodden piece. Even in suits eaten alive by quest for more of nothing worthy, unwilling to dig for that which is affirmation. In restaurants of old fame with deep dark red booths and food delivered and consumed. Tasty as that intoxicating journey through what we'd like to think were better days. Truth of which is likely more in need of some make-up and hair styling than we're willing to submit. Sax is quiet. Unbridled keeps 'til eternity.

Gypsy Song

Going against the grain creates fine predicament. Soggy oatmeal in bowl of alphabet soup with more than twenty six variables. Interpreting unpleasant dialectic can result in a bi-polar conflict shredding being to chilled bone. Airwaves teem with deathly life, wagering vampiric over which will dominate as the gods take vengeance upon our hideous common reflection. Beneath a bridge battered by rain swollen, woman and child rescue. Police chase through riverside. Boy dies in swimming pool, eight adults nearby. Actor falls from grace. Biden scratches forehead. Boss has dinner. Pittolina scratches ass on red carpet. Drunk from Tennessee hills goes on rampage- slaughters seven sheep and three liters of moonshine before passing out in a pig sty where he is devoured in record time for a live meal albeit handicapped by the gin. Cousin of sheriff, apparently prepped to lay down his tin in order to operate the family tommy gun business. Without reflection is a subdivision of action/awareness dichotomy. Possibly not actually dichotomous, but close enough if not being graded. Awareness is a big vest to carry, oft laden with extraneous lead which segues nicely into human condition likely more disease of heft than symptomatic innocuous something or other. Leading to seven billion inquiring minds wants to know of whether uninvited genesis can be retroactively chopped off before birth without creating some sort unwelcome butterfly effect. Something of disturbing nature as time travel has yet to be mastered. Incurable ailment disrupting interplanetary calm. Cause rests easy for now. Effect is a never sleeping response to mundane and inane. Elation and sorrow and rage and love. Open all day every day even Christmas- pipes in when sandman is doing his hell rap thing on depleted rem, resulting in a system naturally running like spawning salmon. Hoping to dodge grizzly ends. Defying odds. Bangin' out bookin' out. Unprecedented notwithstanding. Knowing we're all headed down sometime, post coital seems best anyway. Less preferable avenues around every corner. Awaiting what might follow incinerator. Not an iota of delusion nor false modesty present as declaration of I ain't gettin out that easy is signed. Got my palm read. Can't find the letters in that trough of mush mouth broth. Don't think results were positive. Was told to come back later. I did. One born every minute. Flying against the weather, fucking himself in royal fashion. Lamenting. A dear friend swallows a barrel. Two eardrums splayed staining wooden floors in perpendicular fashion. No bullet recovered. Only dust of what was.

Stealing Home

Man who should never have known himself and likely never did throws himself into fire brimstone cauldron of madness. Bells ring ceaseless from pesky you're only as good as your last type crowd. Lone apparition rattles sabers of his own collection. Stabs outer husk- deflates hyper ego. Autopilot id mistakes breath for anything resembling shovel and ground cover while last of triumvirate sleeps off a disinterested bender, exhausted from copious adjudications whose case files form fusilli towers in the abandoned office. In sickness and in health generates an std to uncontrolled guffaws from invisible guests at a chapel co-opting legend for cheap ape of an erstwhile king. Running through a thread of purple horizon backdrop for a scene from one small step for man however gravity still applies- pulls unwitting to jagged rock at terminal velocity. Downhill picks up jet-pack speed zigzagging off booted tire of failed institution and defiled constitution. A chromosome goes missing. Sends forever into eternity for good. Broken back horse seeks wings though finds years pass in vicissitude with no promise of escape path from purgatorial sentence. Confused dartboard has too many piercings for additional yet holes continue to leak, indicating a condition yet bled dry. A bottomless cliff from even somewhere between, is too close for comfort however is not recognized until after the fact. Accidental descent would have made for a bad day if you believe the papers. Might've been preferable with more context of story line. Relativistic trades blow for blow with objective. Conflict of interest ethos declares no winners. Though preconceived of ulterior motive doesn't necessarily require recusal and the decision rendered appears fair. Washing off gutter stink in vernacular and line breaks which don't follow planning commission guidelines. Come out smelling like rotting rose garden. A scent more lovely not felt for two score plus some. Character portrayed introduces himself to the actor. Only as good as your last doesn't register in marquee laughing to the bank. No matter the depiction so feebly displayed. Scribe catches no such break. Suffering jaundice when seeing corrupted exhibition of release from fractured heart and spilled ink.

Though entirely possible is that it hit too close to a home never to be felt.

Nighttime On A Nickel

What would normally be a stroll through the park isn't so in pitch black. Trash heaps adorn curbsides where tent is housing of choice. Yet to be taken under eminent domain, further pressing into nowhere. Girls in short skirts pass legless veterans stuck on the bottle. High-brow barstools behind a sidewalk grate bellowing warmth over shelter. Where birds fly in winter and sun begins its sleep, lock and key. Sunrise side ain't so lucky, pushed out by forces of mixed emotion. Under every awning, evil sits in mind's eye or in here and now. Beneath each doorway, dissociative, neglected and mad about it pair with plain evil. Strolling Fifth from Maple. Moving west from boarded up, appliance box more comforting than dormitories of angry, insane blood. Ugly alternative throws garbage to the street. Moving towards Pershing Square. Not but five or six blocks. Gauntlet of peddlers seek opportunity for negotiation. A surprising festive spirit surrounds them in what is but one of the evening's off-center spiral stairways through an alternate universe. From a dark piece of wall covering, substantively more than imposing death incarnate stares psychopathic. A laser takes aim and sears my skull upon passing. In my footprint falls the report of his. Where my stride breaks, so too his. Inaccessible is a useless weapon. Gait, tenor and posture portend probable outcome. Rarely off kilter confronted by any storm steps into the square. Scratches small of the back in favor of unsheathed pocket. Caught the drift of rifle-bored intention sends lurker trotting. Moon wink nighttime street scour, intoxicating since memory serves. Fuel for the lady before her name was musically revealed. Even pulse, price of admission. Six hundred sixty six angels and demons struggle for land rights. Eating them all. Sticking to them as a fly on decaying walls. Surgically attached at the hip. Old Greyhound station, once an unsafe beacon to dripping behind the ears is now a 'mart,' most certainly fixed for demolition. Deconstruction is murder though reconstruction, life. Therein lies if not a shoe-in for blue ribbon then certainly in the running for ultimate urban paradox. A dichotomy lost atop heat generating grates as Ferrari ass chicks in thin wrapping strut by, annoyed at the eyesore. An epoch too enticing to set free. Trying to catch what's left before tomorrow. City at night. A better nurse there has never been.

Fluttering Brick Road

Beating butterfly wings creating illusionary tracers could be telltale of chaos or at least a harbinger of events to come barring intervention by a nose twitch scratched in a manner not prescribed by the story set to unfold. Matter of perspective is function of varying circumstance transcending unaware planes of dichotomous notions throwing long balls to the same endzone though airflow is a moving target. Futile is the search for meaning in a maelstrom of exponentiated potential following conception, itself bordering insane given there is no point. Numerous recalcitrant rays drift into the overtly optimistic-attempt to divert attention from the gore of confusion though the graph bluffs its way into infinity on the back end. Behind which a man pulls strings. Ensconced in velvet, fearing discovery. Protests hard absent virility utilizing mind tricks handed down from warriors in a galaxy far far away and more than a bit of decent prophylactic pyrotechnic. Robes always fall. Cloak of invincibility is a transparent tattered rag of masters of no universe yet to stumble upon the negative in that job description. Apparently current events evolved from a twister where dust swirls send roosters headlong into steer. Substituting earthquake would surely produce entirely different rope to pull. Perhaps the sage might still be adorned in emerald, sitting obscure agoraphobic. Cheap antic and platitude of a mediocre card shark carnival barking destiny with sincerity of a palm reader presents a hopeful alternative to wandering aimless for answers. Destiny's a trip of a light bulb sliding through the rails of presage though not unnoticed. Portends carved in stone at some future date while variables shift in a slamdance of celestial violence. Eschews equation of random sampling today, yesterday and tomorrow assuming of course no forecasting smoke and mirror technique at its disposal. Committing suicide before recognized, a kid of Dutch origins relegates vain to advanced mathematics which will forever miss a corner piece of the puzzle or perhaps never encounter the enigma of useless though nevertheless intriguing paradox to begin with. Hens now sound dawn's alarm. And the arc of the butterfly is forever altered.

Jettisoned

My beard cuts the wind. Ice sends blood to boil-holds onto the past though what constitutes yesterday is up for debate. Dream is coastline yet to be stricken by thunderous gale. Ukuleles in odd tunings play turn out the lights the party's over. Pounding beat over which the orchestra cannot fly is either restless leg syndrome or cracking of hollow stone. Gutted and splayed drips yoke not rinsed by henchmen from below surface chop who for reasons unknown as tomorrow, seem to have a hard on for me. Leave a trail of geological ova to closed case. Working class mynahs squawk a love song longing for exiled patron. Virtue rarely finds shelter in wings of unrecognized greatness. Carried on shoulders of gods who but shrug when queried as to why expedited departure guidelines are being followed. Stomped is hope for an alternative outcome to pregnant cloud burst which has no choice in the matter. Walking barefoot over hot coals apparently fails to impress rainforest laughing at unharmonious that never matches sweet aromatic wild boar spinning on spits any better than a melody which didn't quite come together on swing-sets either. Or the carver chipping away at sorrowful koa not at all interested in being chiseled but lack choice in furniture design. And now the wind cuts my beard. Fast forward time zone filling ventricle with driving spikes through dream which by any other reference is a nail head yet to meet the hammer. I met him. He turned tail, jetting off with a flip of fin. Perhaps a sign from where heart dubiously eased in what would eventually present as a maze leading headlong into molten ledges chopping at a love so pure as to defy natural order. Missing gorilla in the room left rolling in dry sand atop a needle in haystack. Wished adieux by denizens of the deep behind rowdy three decade injury. Unnamed degenerate characters must have a role though it's buried in obtuse dialogue similar to paper-thin lie of I do followed by opaque legalese reams of I don't. Tossed into comfortable digs in a bubble I refuse to pop. Preferring instead something of an organic implosion. The new land lubber ol' lady couldn't care less either. Glacial white out travels east. It's cold here. That it's not a revelation is proof I'm repeating myself. Familiar artificial turf which began taking its toll on joints when destiny birthed its bite.

Under The Light

Questions of fortitude present a feeble case under imposition of incredulous third degree. Sweaty palms are likely indications of trepidation if not genetic misstep though it could just be heat emanating from a rage intractable as a Kennedy organ hand-washed in gin. Stars illuminating smiles somewhere. Legitimate is questionable. Smells like malt spirit. Not buying it is denying primacy of just smile be happy go fuck off somewhere. Cleaver strikes brilliantly accurate, splitting hemispheres. The world is painted numb petulant. Telescopic intrusion through forensic sightless spurs additional mindless meanderings as it views the previous in disbelief, proving Heisenberg may have had a point. Ubiquitous invisible hands-free stare chokehold. Immovable unnamed power prodding depression to cubicle and basement noose. Reflexive scrutiny impressed by its discovery peers yet closer. Boiling point pushed further into red-zone. Tighter and tighter they watch as thoracic squeezes. A new variable is poisoned human stroke to the painting following strenuous observation whose results are then examined. Too many hands in the soup ladle the thing to death with keen analysis of obvious and multitude fixes for one problem which isn't. Orb in question is nothing more than attempt at a straight shot boomerang return though never connecting with home following initial introduction to the grand illusion in what is more paradoxical truism though once presented itself as conundrum of theory. Spinning wheel continues to spit high tension wire across the stage despite uncomfortable silence of the non-sequitur or one simply spin-doctored to death. Running out of space is a line snaking at direction of angular confines creating a ball of wire twine bursting its periphery from every circular tangent though intent was a different geometric pattern and even failed attempt by anonymous sources for a complete circle are exposed dangling participles at each end of a rapidly expanding contraction which is being watched carefully. To slow death. Of course like a northeastern storm, there's but a sliver of a chance I'm overthinking a touch or at least channeling a boastful song from a right coast bird who sings what left resonance never could.

Contrived

Transcending bounds set by conventional standards. Invoking instead laws of other planes or more aptly what could be found elsewhere though likely show in disguise. Invisible evidence lost the scent to transient hair on the back of neck ephemera. Hippos take mud baths in turkey followed by a eucalyptus swatting that hurts so good. Pyramids are on jacks. Sold for a song by a new regime with western attitudes towards gentrification though lacking skill of appraisal. Highest and best use calculations computed under Sharia law point to six dozen virgins for every man if zoning exemptions are passed creating the galaxy's largest castle of area rug genuflecting pedophilia with state of the art acoustics capable of doubling prayer to ten kneels per day in hopes for a faster trip to promise though a cluster bomb would save them callous knees. Short term nickel and dime concern of tourism loses the bidding by hard-on under robe lubeslide. Egypt falls into the Red Sea. Never heard from again. In other news, righteous rhythm explodes underfoot calling even the most devout unbeliever to reconsider as notes of faith of superlative grace linger in mirage air encapsulated with song to an enigma. Mercury between the fingers. Breaking of sound barrier deflates soaring balloon of maybe just too thin skinned to keep the faith brother but thanks for the prayer. Striking a bus with no ill intent- wreck the conveyance. Scores injured in the wake of broken science of collision. Opens doors to new fields of study though fingers have scratched through most capable heads leaving only square pegs for quite a round hole. Class cancelled until a qualified nuttier 'an a fruitcake professor is pulled from beneath fire hazard fir and sobered up from nog spiked with sopor speedball type concoction lacking the speed part. Stepping outside the fence of a world of sand empire into ruddy vocals of waits struggling for melody in what is about as close to perfection as is tolerable in *civilized* society, by which I mean *uncivilized* but as the italicized is a direct derivative of that lacking stressful punctuation then by long forgotten axiom theorem or postulate and given that civilized is nothing more than euphemistic feel good then so too by extension is the twin bookended by paraphrase. Avoiding confusion as is apparent is a call for commonality in vernacular. All a long hard road to short soft simple- civilized ain't. Shoulda started there as that's where it ends though the clicking keyboard sends me off to orgasmic heights from which I'm unable to pull myself but for new word contradicting that which blows my sail skyward. Not necessarily a bad thing. Drunk on the moon or drunk in public are both intoxicating though an occasional trip back to the land scholarship relegated to gravity keeps feet on the ground. Thorazine dumps into water supply replacing fluoride. Nobody complains but for cloudy visions all too real. Way too close to conventional standards and 'civilization' shamelessly imprisoning body and mind. And for fuck's sake, I'm back on earth. Note the comma to prove it. Fly-by over an illusionist who's said to make water dance his tune cancelled until further notice.

Flashes

Sea hunters dive bomb abalone blackened water. Ocean air unleashes a dagger attack inducing an uncontrollable shiver. There's a hole in my heart and it's you. Think that's a song but what the fuck. If the shoe fits I guess. Damn I'm loaded with old material. Must be the broken bricks at base of the structure. Barely this side of melting to quicksand. And a dog wails break a leg to passing fire engine- unequivocally predicting a fractured outcome. Balls in the air are actually bowling kind streaking violent. Irons in fire serve only to brand with scarlet letter when we all know it happened on someone else's watch. Manufactured in Switzerland with parts from China. Delivered by Greek. Not sure any of this is germane though loose filament bulbs ain't shining all so well. One can hear flash misfire. It becomes rapidly apparent what drives the truck down this black hole of decaying foundation. Sucking all who must toil upon her soil into dilated blank stare throughout life in order to keep streets entrails-free as spontaneous suicide becomes new national sport and is catching on quickly. Utilizing what has become synonymous with sheep going over a cliff. Sniffing the preceding ass on decades long trudge to a merciless track of Norwegian death rock would rightly sound cliché though this footwear also fits like orange juice and steak knives. In deference to avoiding such vice, let's just call us, ummm...sheep. Got nothing better. Walking across croc water with no old men to clear a throughway. The reptiles eat well. Frogger plays you in an uncomfortable changing of the guard. Jamie's cryin'. Bitch better not short the amp. Additional electrical problems in the unit could result in loss of occupancy, though vacant has never been the issue. All too present unfortunately breeds with echo and forecast to fuck the calendar up but good. Making an appointment requires a smartphone laughing at the dumbass trying to manipulate its electronic handcuff. Collared in the marina. Like still married kinda collared with a shock device you continue to apply to your own skin just long enough to lose the leash- doleful evermore. Carnivorous very same thinning foundation claims responsibility which then, further demonstrating its spite, regurgitates to wallow ponder awhile. I'm fairly certain history repeats here too. More dusty script. Maybe it's in those damn wilting bricks playing connect the dots with past present and future again. Had a thought but lost it. Where were we? Smokin out with rest of the flock. Stomach woes non-existent as I take my turn at brim of flaming chasm.

Counting Bleeps

Promise in the dark is narcoleptic. Sleep deprived at that. Drifting into fantasy of what could have been is indolent man's excuse for inaction in addition to depressing the system to sleep. Tomorrow is a crack pipe. Ghosts are apparitions in pedestrian jargon. Attacking sandman with moderate prejudice. Awake is a bus transfer to internal combustion not strumming in tune with the heavens. A penny from which could be one earned or perhaps a litmus test of ethic. Seeding what comes with inaction but glued to expression above and beyond the call of duty though duty calls with lofty expectation. Several ways off the snowy mountain. None involve travel further upward-guarantees disappointment from surfeit fly-by-night patrons below and a chuckle from judgment circling in a weak impersonation of bird of prey on the hunt. Shuteye stopped midway between blinks. What could have been is laced with two grams of happy. Immeasurable quantitative evaluation of textile unraveling at the seams diagnoses incessant rumination over what light might exist in the shadow. Put another way, someone ain't snoring which is sleeping off the above reiteration. Roller coaster elation lost its draw in nonsensical ambition though the artificial clanking of danger keeps lines full of impatient white knuckles. As well as the hoping for respite from said youthful exuberance paradoxically accompanied by a faint recollection of simple. Perhaps escape for a moment the hurried pile of drafts to be signed after performing a crate of novenas which don't recognize my kind anyway. The taxman cometh. Collections probably better this year. Money burns a hole in Capitol pockets faster than clap on a Marine's first Bangkok excursion. This is my rifle. This is my gun...shooting off mouth. Spraying staccato without concern for line of fire. Raging at universal which doesn't much care but to drop a couple more straws to humor spitting camels. They hand the script off to their big brother who proceeds to begin location hunt but finds authentic too hot to handle. Instead choosing comfortable digs for the reel which eludes caged beast screenplay, missing plotline by a full degree of latitude. Film flat-lines, going straight to video although there are no assurances that sticking with the product as intended would have done any better. Maybe the French'll buy it. Anybody still laughing with Jerry not at him, certainly is a candidate for bidders' tent at upcoming bridge auction. Pie in dead skies is accretion is breath before slumber. Dilutive foreshadow of meaningless may never come passes itself off as vital statistic. Is a thief. Stealing night its loot. Rising to the fall that opens startled eyes which remain no lower than before the cruel tease of bed's oath. Promising more attention to spiritual detail. In the dark. Crossed fingers seem to go unseen. Type a jerkoff dies flipping digits which add to nil once the accountants take a crack at it. Traversed scabby picket line of religious transformative lies past previously sworn curfew. Crossed fingers have same impact as bloody crucifixes on tatted torsos of horizontal urban warrior type. Tired as a lone whore on a troop ship though for some reason can't sleep. And have no clue as to why.

What If

Cascading waterfalls tumble over the precipice for no apparent physical purpose. Cantilevered subsets of self infatuated is always in search of an angle. Rock and roll and all things in between bouncing off my roof. A horn blows to alternate destination unknown. Laughing out of the tube the notes soar towards a hundred doves dancing atop a power line next to a strung out set of sneakers. The line's abuzz with rhythm. Cops beat down their walks. Giraffes run backward around unnatural enclosures though fanged carnivore is out of sight, of mind. Waxing somewhat poetic though only scratching the surface of the tune thumping off the street. Odor of the alleys. I don't get it blares from behind the rope. There's a pizza grease stain on my shirt. The back. Greco roman wrestling was sold to the Turks. Mesopotamia bustles under my turbocharged rug and a donut of all things captures thought. Opportunity knocks me off my feet. Leaves me where it found me. Ghetto kids are skippin' a masterful rope like you never see portrayed. Blood on the tracks keeps more viewers stoned. Another kid slaughters three dragons. Two Cokes. Polishes off a box of Pop-Tarts while Elvis makes his final appearance. Kennedys rise and are shot again. This time irrefutably from the depository. Photos courtesy of the grassy knoll. Charlie got his recording contract. Helter Skelter never bled though the desert parties are still the shit. Brian Wilson sings of memories. Not mournful wishes to blow in the wind. Jim Jones spikes his sugar water with L-25 and the world undulates about a vortex not all that interested in sucking in new guests. A sommelier took my coffee order. Brought the wrong blend. There's a coffee stain on his shirt. The back. Snapping to something but can't tell what it is. Could tell but then well. Nah. Can't tell. We never fought a land war in Asia. This message is a paid endorsement. Atypical cold front is keeping fingers tapping for warmth or just to syncopate the weather-indifferent shakes. There's a single light manifesting its presence. Kindred illumination hides from sight as agreed upon in a don't call me I'll call you sort of pact. They're coming faster than I can mangle them. Racing through the lobes to hopeful ends atop a heap of virtuous meander. Think the roses don't appreciate the chill either. Half a joint is soon to be toasted. I listen to a smokin' joint. Shred limits with a samurai thrust. Smack my head on the floor. Pen rollicking nonsensical. I smiled today.

Self-Adjudicated

An unadulterated mess has arrived at my feet- chews gum into my soul like a gnawing nebulous that defies tangible. Lowered expectations seem to be a common thread in evaluation of purpose in effort. Watching a series of numbers float by without definition but that I prescribe. Unfortunate turn of events sets me back though back could be front if looking in opposing mirrors. A trait not typical of my ventures though an old dog can learn new tricks of not too lazy or simply stuck on spreading waste product to the world at large which often seems so small and getting smaller. Can't abide judgment of conditions as a fair trial. Typically judge jury and executioner sit in my lap. Hanging judge at that. Hanging to distant howls of like wolves seeking companionship though the bitches are in hiding though maybe I'm hiding from the bitches. Wandering off into my lair to occupy space and time with clickety clack. Serving up a pound of flesh per ounce of energy. Running out of ounces to spare. A trip to the pharmacy is a balm of no lasting relief. Retching in a diatribe about medicinal nausea plasters a cracked portrait with many voices. Myopic views through a set of binoculars is an inaccurate suggestion of one eyed blindness. Only the one eye has twenty-twenty vision though sees everything through rose colored glasses in evasion of reflection that proves too depressing to explicate however back-tracing from the outcome presents some interesting arguments about preceding events. Blacktop melting into a mirage throwing apparitional vapor into a crowded pot is sucking mojo to the marrow. So deep in own rhythm don't know how to make time making time. Round ass swaying with the step-down tuning just how I like it. Bobbing and weaving on a sidewalk meant for two. Uninhibited is clamped and gagged- indirectly correlated to time in service though I could have that backwards. Copperhead strike atop the boot results in depleting finances or emergency room multiple choice with ten possibilities turning bed inside out in a stream of Dilaudid. Do with me what you will. There's no chemical leftovers for the road. An unfortunate truth when invisible is more than a dull throbbing in the heart but an ubiquitous stab like pain in the side in the heart in the chattering smirk-ravens cawing snickers on a branch previously unknown to science though aestheticians got hands around the metaphysical neck long ago. When added up comes to howling in the darkness in search of the next forever to step inside my shadow on a sidewalk meant for two or in a bed with a silhouette dreaming me into existence. Calling for a level of compromise that makes me feel as if all the above is just wasted space. Like the hole that cannot be filled without gunning down reprobate narcissist in the fogged window seat. Like a desert succumbing to the wishes of so many rainstorms that all arid roaming creatures drown in subsurface mud. An outline of cactus which fails to weather the torrent itself.

Flicking Ashes

Last of life's pleasures are calling my name from a well lighted place which always sets me back a few steps. Respiring in deep concentration to the asymmetrical wheeze. The sun gently stroking chilling conditions. Red white black toxic box sneers death's smile. National banner with a socialist tax stamp indicating complicity among fascists of alternate lineages. Among polluted bloodstream in taking noxious fumes of post industrial man and machine. In quest for balance has tilted the world out of orbit. Quality/quantity relativistic driving coach in opposite directions on various days though no signs are posted but for the Bic at hand. In effect, negate time consuming waltzes with no convincing bend to seal the dance floor. Colorless passes in surreal pauses which never stop too long as I light another to continue value assessments. Compulsive itch is scratched on keys though whether they open doors is another matter. Coughing up dissolution is expectorated of a different color. Hazy trail through cobwebs trying to reach conclusion. Increasing recently retreated gut wrench back to pre-treaty hostilities will come over my dead body. Flick. Inhale. Blow. Inextricably linked lethal logic goes silent into dark dopamine before continuing assault on that transitory wind of post-modern neutral popping straight through the gears-stripping the first couple. Bringing it down a notch from redline into what most would call unbearable but I consider a walk in an autumn park with aid of another. Realizing smoke never put a gun to my head. Life can't claim like innocence. Another wrung down the ladder with the next drag is a ball and chain to questionable ends. Hormonal animosity again revs the engine. Slide draws back. Round chambered. Time for another flick. Murderous stress is plotting to off me. Probably signifies need for another scrawl. Recipe- a gallon stomach-chew eased by fruit of thy womb cannabis- roll to taste- and sacramental burn of chemically enhanced subsidy. Shutting the motor down to roll with the lady. Just making sure I've all the right toys in place. Brutality is shelter from the storm door opened to an unprepared suitor. Look ma- low blood pressure. Agonizing is departure from pseudo tranquil brought by full fledged affirmative denial despite it killing you. Markings of the Reich marching me to the showers as Madame Butterfly plays so sincerely sorry. A hideous train ride never to be forgotten. Even if it takes winding jet fume pattern over emotion to reach final destination. All certainly unreasoned ratiocination but any glue to stick straight dope on the page will be adhered to. Choice exists where none did. Black white red box of Reds stoking flame of yellow hexagon. Whatever it takes lights another.

Hooray For Checkered Boulevard

Cult of personality lacks an economical diet. Is there another variety? Varying in degree in an even climate. Opening Pandora's box. Sea to sea dissected purple colors. Corrupted dialectic which seems so dichotomous as to wonder if they're too close for comfort. Communal rhetorical issue as I'm fairly certain of the story I'm sticking with. Warfare atop sacred sites of wanton massacre of red and their herds. Civilization shredded disprove civil. Textbook judo tossed theory of progress denying DNA with hard hip-throw breaking playbook backbone. Distributed like CIA crack urban destruction campaign behind euphemistic saber rattling. Canyons-stream-rivers-plains-towns fighting headwinds whence Washington led us to freely destroy hate worship at tip of king's failure. Invade. Pollute. Fractionalized from beginning is the only way to control unless your press secretary is Goebbels. Prevailing wisdom-less directives suggest distinct possibility. Overweight divided has developed diabetes and needs to tone down sugar promises made of stevia. Ok corrals culture icon transfiguring into transformers with multiple advanced weapon systems. Hollywood has no culpability. Just ask it for a wholly biased view. Recently released samplings imply a large number of actors adorning that toxic stage. Waiting list for slots is anticipated hope- homicidal optimism to the horror of expectation. Congressional pages pour over pages of if not illegal it is now. Barney Frank pours over pages over pages. Depleted legislators eat cottage cheese- read decisions from sign language translator to maintain radio silence of inattention to it's always in the details. Now black-listed but for his little black book hired sizzling heat for interpretation. Big tit blonde with tight ass likes horses and commandos. Hates war and mean people. Flashbulbs immediately capture what's left of her soul-wiping out any chance at subterfuge as fevered queries shoot from all corners as to the meaning of events and where are the finger foods. What's the bimbo's phone number was a close third though Piers Morgan got the jump on her. Formerly right leaning had a platinum moment which is pretty much redundant but readers know of that tendency. Fox switches favored station in life to CNN. Got yet more confused. Jumped from a first story window. Busted implants minutes before a lucrative Playboy offer hit her flaxen phone which advised a higher floor. Drunken distinguished fat bastard from Massachusetts will now be heard puking up stream water and placenta- summarily shot by Capitol police under strict orders from chain of command with broken links. Never had a dream come true. People say I think too much. Thank god I trashed antisocial media newspaper and TV. In the mood grizzly with no fear of roaring up fucking up and repeating the process. Think I enunciated so much in body of text though memory is lacking. Undue stress is watching helpless as starless cut-outs are lifted to papal heights. I can only imagine what the Catholics think.

Smelling The Lotus

Obliterated in a tornado yarn-storm circling about my universe like all constellations were cinched to conscription in Orion's belt. Escaping the vapid soil in a void entreating with rolling thunder. Departing is such sweet brilliance. Concurrently aloof in the unapproachable sense while sucking impeachable despicability into my vortex. Confronted with precepts which burn like a funeral pyre from the corner of my eyes tearing to the smoky confines of introspection running wild in the streets with unencumbered recalcitrance. Traveling far and wide from witless action of anything but dimwitted which is not the contradiction it appears to be. On perma-hold with an associate professor of you're fucked up- take these. Becoming more arid in a rainforest of record downfall breaking branches. Ripping lichen from the glue that blinds. Telling lurid tales which are nothing but delusional recollections which overpowering superego further redacts. Never fooled though oft taken is exacting blood curdling rage on his only nemesis. Shards of what should have been lacerate golem before it. Existential crisis is preparing an ambush on spirited neurology with control of the epoch at stake. Slink through the soaked wasteland with tongue tasting the sugar air in search of something with a bit more substance though can't seem to find much but for meanderings of odd spirit somewhere which is nowhere according to digital coordinates though technological advances could be bouncing its signal from data centers in Mumbai further entangling scorched earth with spawning a really confused bastard of ink. Ephemera who is always there. Enigma whose tangled linguistic destruction is a trove of untold potential which isn't strong enough in that in no bounds nothing is not possible. Slipping out of character into another's for a bit is as comforting fascination as looking at the crass on the other side of the fence. It's always greener until they're jumping from windows with bottles of Wild Turkey. High and mighty until the iphone snaps light's out. Proselytizing partisan taking a strong right turn though a more liberal stance with fecund page. Seems that constricting belt is centered around brazen affairs of misstate and the licentious sod in which they plant stakes. Bipartisan foray has no lines to pill box amity and Jim Beam diplomacy though something can be arranged. Setting myself to explode on contact would seem to be current state of affairs of which there are none to speak but this intoxicated interwoven mess of ether speed depress- release casting a gray pall over ambivalent tan mass which is only marginally less objectionable than contented square boxes. Stroking her softly while she asks for something a bit rougher. The dude abides. Salacious intermingling leaving fingers smelling nothing like roses though the bloom is unmistakable.

Upchuck

Running on an empty tank in car with no motor but plenty of oil gliding down a highway which breathes in blacktop rhythm of rising steam which is all an illusion but who's to say? Red crows are trailing a black hawk down a ravine for a meal on the house. An undulating field of weeping willows crying the blues. Dusty old mining town with a general store specializing in nothing. Raucous saloon fronted by a hitching post tie-dyed like a dead-head. Nobody uses it and its colors melt like ice cream in the scum though the imprint remains leaving the tragic posts to wallow without purpose. Same as before only agonizingly anonymous. Denying a hard time in deeply veiled eastern mystical tongue with which I'm unfamiliar is telling me that because the broom can sweep there is a newly found Zen monk donning a Pro-Club t-shirt. You got me. Though I don't answer to anything but expletive anyway. Regardless, it has been suggested that recent moderation is setting a new low bar. Abjectly petrifying is being accused of even keel risking more of the same which will most definitely throw me off balance and may result in everything squaring up- the second most petrifying thing I can imagine or maybe it's just a subset of even keel they're accusing me of after initiating unwelcome contact which is redundant if you stand in my shoes that thank god you don't or you'd have big soles to fill with minimal expectation or else you might actually get somewhere and ruin everything you've worked so hard to destroy. Which all comes back to why I'm cool at the moment but you have to make a hard right or soft left. Comes down to a ballsy girder-laying act which either confirms assumed stupidity of the human condition or fulfills a funambulist dream. One man's fantasy is another's tombstone. Declining any interviews for fear of making myself clear instead of veiling emotional well being in vaguely surreal old westerns and feigned sagacious mumbling of a temporary sociopath brought to be through extraneous contact with tranquil. Feel me? Pulling over to do some tripping with the red rocks and nowhere else to be. I hear peyote will enlighten- bring you closer to whatever holiness oversees this stuff. Puke but enlighten.

What's more illustrative than knowledge gained while upchucking the bullshit we've been fed all these years.

Follow Doesn't Succeed

Tapping out seven seconds in the first round after losing sensation in my fingers. Can't find a damn thing worth writing about but can't stop the flailing for fear of permanent nerve damage or something taking on the simulacra of an impaled muse. Could be repeating myself within my own structure though that's probably redundant as the point seems self evident. Watching the city flow through crisp gusts which tend to warm more than chill. Pulling on a pharmaceutical device which is now actually used for medicinal purposes. Getting old sucks. Especially for the supposedly in mid-range of stochastic models types. Extraneously sanguine is the mere consideration of any possibility that numerator is going to tip the scale whose base is lilting anyway. Further- holding no apparent counteractive affect which might result in a naturally less abhorrent set of circumstances though equilibrium doesn't have a letter to delineate it within the equation so therefore has no impact on the dynamic and any reference thereto redacted. She'll get hers eventually. Never in fear but always fearful is an uptight twat. Especially if she's holding the marbles and divining rod. Casting a white glow over blackened hill and dale is a faint hint of rhapsodic aria. Seems a bit early in the show for the rotund to take on her clichéd task. Then again those extrapolative models are massive calculations which consider only masses. Individual indiscretion is an unwanted pregnancy or a missing component of unique predictive value which is of no value to billions of fluttering wings. Although portentous is no longer deemed a moral disposition when there's a plate before you in the moment which will soon be another that will have children of its own until there's no more space for any additional moments. And the children wallow in piles of refuse while crop fields are dust. But then the calculations don't adjust for persons singular but people plural- could be interpreted as nothing but integer greater than one yet nothing could be further from the truth. Ninety is either the percentage of relations that sour or the number of assholes one will find if examining thirty. Seems reasonably successive to succumb to base linear mathematics which is an unloved subject around some of these parts though irreconcilable differences don't divorce children. Forty three going ninety. Kilter teeing off. Skewed statisticians impersonating Quasimodo. Hypnotic analytical methodology. Man pillaging man cradle to grave and back. There are no innocents. Collateral damage is either heart break or future transgression whose ticket got punched in a thankfully premature gesture. Nah. I can't find a fucking thing to say however I'm sure I can add a convenient non-sequitur though that ruse hasn't a chance of holding up a liquor store let alone a bank.

Major Tom

Trippin' off to a stupid idea with zero chance of a non imbroglio crashing down like hundred foot waves leaving me stranded in the deep blue which as a side note, is untenable due to a thirty year old grievance which obviously holds a grudge. Yeah like I was gonna leave mango and coconut but for threat of emotional injury or spiritual death and I'm still not sure. Sticking to a cakewalk in the sky as the pie's been exhausted yet tastes as sweet as it stings like infuriated fire-ants at a contentious reunion barbeque. Another dream sent to the infirmary with no real reason to believe it will leave but on a slab. Stacking on repetitive motion to the point of inconclusive ends however at least it's familiar surroundings. Interested lately in seeing Styx. Ultimate fear of man is unknown though it is true that many have spoken of the evil waters and is cited in many texts so I'm not quite sure it's a complete stranger though I don't rely on second or third or a hundredth printing but have insatiable desire to digest trivia like it was loaded with omega 3 fatty acids and I actually gave a fuck about omega 3 fatty acids. So Styx. Yeah, well- sort of figuring with so many good things being reported about that which lies above that perhaps it's an overbought commodity and maybe it might be better to start at the bottom. Or the drifting currents which get you there anyway. No need to bounce off a pitchfork. But anyway, seems like a more interesting place even if all the stories are true. You heard of a whorehouse in heaven? Can't even spill the seed. How's the ferryman making out? Rules can build one incorrigible miscreant and where not prosecutable will be poster child for new regulation. Won't bow to icon nor invisible faith something in its incalculable sky acts plausibly hospitable (or tangible authority for that matter with a gunpoint exemption). Though go with god I say. Wish I could. Or even have him stop by and demand penance- in which case I'd reconsider my galvanized position though I'm still not clear on what it is I'm remorseful for but things beyond the interest or time constraints of any great power. Instead I hand a dollar when I can. An ear at least for a second or two. Act courteous to the waitresses and busboys. And can look forward to eternity in fire if you believe that sort of thing which I do in a sense as I plan to have myself immolated upon departure which is neither here nor there but felt it worth mentioning. So. Have I mentioned I'm a misanthrope and hear me roar? Important interlude in that I have a kindergarten level equation: the species sucks therefore its people suck so inhaled indignities and pain they would inflict on another therefore renders them abhorrent and likely the most vile creature ever to hike any terrain on any plane in any solar system or galactic formation which all really means man hurts man without provocation therefore man sucks. Successive remains and adapted reptiles on distant islands present a pretty solid argument though some claim a jury of twelve was involved in a scheme to make their contribution larger than it really was but why throw stones? Besides, I wasn't there but am still counting on wells to get me back for a more complete assessment of events or at least pimp for an invite to the dinner. Forcing him to choose another path so that we could all stop this communal masturbation and get on with life whether the hard evidence is offered into the records or not. For sickness and in health 'til devotion you find. I ain't finding any anytime soon. Been head-faked too many times to buy it....oh yeah, the imbroglio. Earth to Danny: no nefarious action when under the influence of medication nor shifts in planetary formation. Covers a lot of territory in blanketed proscription.

Call Bluff And Raise

Trying to skip past obstacle which isn't currently blocking anything. Locked in not atypical self reflection which is lacking introspective byline. Playing connect the dots which never seem to come together with some though some aren't paying attention. Dropping a tab to another zone would be a welcome distraction though heading to Las Palmas or the boardwalk questioning human reek for who's holding is a quick way to nowhere nowadays. Sunset motels are strewn with cheap Hollywood keepsakes made in Taiwan or Taipei or Senegal for all I know. Lightly rehabbed windowsills decked out in attic trash rather than windowpane which got washed out for the most part. And god knows what I might do under the influence of get the fuck out of my trip anyway. Sticking to inexorable internalized debate is gummy calculus which never touches itself however continues to grind the mechanisms. Can't let it go is a muse that's begging for sleep I won't provide. Draped in a velvet robe, I beat her into submission to which she'll never submit. Just kidding, sweetheart. I know better. So sitting in Seoul west wondering why I'm getting mad-dogged by a bad driver sipping coffee speaking in tongue two seats away. Laser through the back of his head blank as the state I might have once visited with venom and joy though the tank's now low and I'm too old for this shit which is probably repetitive so I won't repeat it. Regardless, can't drive shows his cards before the river runs. Scratches his nose. Looking away as the front to the new Korean conflict overplays its hand. Loving cards though weak bluffs bore me. Besides, I'm blinded by the noise I recall stating so I won't reiterate it. Silent stare speaking volumes tells me everything I need to know and occasionally can set me back a few years. I was a prick back a few years.

Blood On The Track Marks

A street lined with decorative innards of what could never be paved with organic solutions. Plagued by vacuity of utopian science paying no heed to echoes cranked to eleven without distortion. Lines roll by like a staccato hoover swept up in a tweaking cyclone of blood on scabby tracks. Craving red meat. Burnt to gristle crisp so that infuriating granola-munch is out of earshot. Ripping flesh to the bone while amber eyed grave dancers drop visine intended for a different high than the on life kind who preach abstinence between B-12 shots and colonics. Flying buds stuffed in my pipe though I prefer paper. Particular interest are Sunday crosswords which don't seem so antagonistic though perhaps the red herring is in the christening. But then I can't decipher wheat from rhetorical cacophony of dead not buried chafe so why bother paying heed to the calamine doused nut behind the transparent curtain for he rants unremittingly though the tired bark is increasingly patient and the bite awaits purpose? Waning years which began before birth have been in a downtrend ever since and are showing signs of unhinged portals or rusty nails or whatever allegorical reference suits you. Accusations of pessimistic appetite are met with a wink and earth shuttering shrug of a god whose name is now used in vain though am fairly certain that wasn't an obsession atop Olympus however I'm unmistakable as a one way street that I'm anything but an expert witness on leanings of marble arches. Crowds leave me Mexican jumping bean at a chili cook-off type anxious yet crowds are the norm so reevaluating all positions is taking first step in thousand mile inquisition confined to a ten mile diameter. Apparently all answers worthy of enquiry are either explicit scripture or just one stroke up on a migraine of a scorecard indicating don't question intent or speciously bestowed which won't are holding a commanding lead going into the back nine. Texts spread open like prom queens so often as to question whether infinite monkeys in the endless galaxy are poking holes in every text ever written. New and improved good book or books in this case for sale as a set or in an omnibus addition. Published by random house or deliberate shack.

Detached from the debate is disengaging the crutch in plan b which really deserves a better grade though why quibble? Korean can't drives (redundant- yea, I got it) fuck the curve up for the whole class. Just smile and be happy is a wonderful slogan for the miserable cultural hijacker though is something I frown upon. Then again too much information is a sure trip to the land of hypnotic nod. A place sounding entirely more comfortable than a brick of ice which will be my resting place as a result of global warming that caught a cold. Misanthropic tumors are searching for reason while utter disconnect is seeking nothing but a little chemical romance which contrary to conveniently deaf popular opinion, can be far less damaging than the fleshy kind.

Upstream

Selling out to everything while looking for something to buy. Nebulous whatever hitherto unattainable and as its ambiguity implies, could be the colloquial snake coiled before me and I'd never know. It's fucking nebulous! Fairly simple geometric progression from there to here and it's none too reassuring. Look it up. Gagging at thought of continuation of the nothing that I persist in accomplishing. Rage management adjudication is yet to have been issued in court of law however they might consider taking it up for public safety purposes. Of course I'd hop the fence with a fanged sneer or so history suggests which should have no impact on current proceedings however there are none on the docket anyway. Nevertheless is a best of three proposition. Winning hand is definition of loser. Might appear to be yet more haziness run amok though there's nothing chipping away at the painstakingly disintegrated calculus. Clotted inclinations are congealing in a treacherous quarry filled with skeletal remains of dejected decomposition. A wrinkled chasm not to be explored alone or at least not without a supersized herring trail. Evidence you were once there to allay any vague recollective concerns reached when early onset dementia intersects a potentially infuriating war of words between déjà vu and recurring nightmare indiscernible due to fugue though responsibility has yet to be officially assigned as witness testimony is vague at best. Wild salmon writhing upstream bouncing off rocks deposited by malefactor gods intent on demanding effort to find the promised land or softer waters just for a laugh. Ground to a fine red mist. Fighting the tide which is admittedly trite but for good hackneyed reason. Crashing into those same rocks where rivers once flowed unabated and spawning fish had a fair chance. Taking a thousand stitches without a laugh track except for the mynahs screeching which I like to think is sniggering with me rather than at me though the doves are comatosed on tryptophan. Said before I have often been designated delusional. It hasn't changed in forty years plus some. It ain't gonna adjust in a stream of questionable consciousness though perhaps a couple more smacks into jetty boulders will be the straws that snap the overplayed camel's wheezing back. Always an oasis with water, shade and figs invisible for the sand-drifts which could either hold the lost ark or a cheap facsimile thereof among the bone sacrificed in the search. Will any of us live to find a reviving splash? Or are we just jerking off to the same tune that rendered Cobain brain splatter with notoriously poor gastrointestinal health which parenthetically of course only matters before the fact though the meaning of it all escapes me? An inopportune yet arguably fortunate confluence of events in the larger scheme as search for meaning in a toxic quagmire with no apparent time signature is subject to change without logic nor universal malice of forethought. Could be nothing more than a pissed off insect deceptively painted like abandon. Nowhere to hide from truth which stings like a sharp stick in the eye however is far more favorable than seeking guidance in tunnel vision of a condor awaiting your demise. Ringing patient for carrion you will be before ever finding that pot of gold or apple on the sacred tree. Catching surreptitious glimpse of eve sans fig leaves could be arranged however payment is required upfront and in fact, both honest misinterpretations and sham misdirects are common so the reference could be nothing more than allusion to a serpentine introduction which would certainly suck though the death would undoubtedly be less painful than emasculating berating which near invariably precedes a blood bath that never washes off. A planet too small in stature to handle two, unleashing pestilence though chapter and verse are most definitely out of context. The whole of which is entirely more promising once defining the abyss- the aforementioned unknown keeping me up at night which is no longer unclear however narcoleptic episodes symptomatic of the larger issue remain unabated- call into question the broad assumptions which are really no more than bogus anecdotal yarns. An insatiable hunger for a straight road to redemption for which I can never collect the savings loses its appetite. Quicksand road to Styx is underfoot. Wherever it steps. Bashing the salmon on its stony bed while desire for existence suffers a massive drop in large-scale polls of broad samplings not to mention landslides burying any procreative desire. And opposites cease to attract. And a jocular rain is hard falling. Hip boots and oar sales scrutinized for price gouging.

Edgy

Trying hard to amplify disquiet through darkness holding no torch. Unsure which arrow shall be loosed from the abundant quiver- not quite the blessing it might seem. Master of all is often jack-off of none. Drying beds of inexplicably arid emotional overload nearing the cliff's edge. Unable to expound upon grand delusion which must be the case as leather clad intelligentsia says so. As a wobbly world off its rocker. Painfully pleased with exclusion from the club as preprogrammed historical hash marks bear witness to planting of acceptance beneath murk so as not to dis fragile componentry with deteriorating inertia and premature bouts of dementia stumbling over its own languid mass. Losing faculties before they're interviewed. Dismissing absurdly hopeful drifting as impossible reverie while holding out optimism cross-currents will fall upon my seas before the wretched ponds drain scum over my final sentence. Suffocating under the pressure of all I can't enunciate. Clogged passages blocking any possibility for potentially amicable solutions. And still they scream. In horror of that which precedes inevitable. In vindictive laughs dripping tears of joy from angels of no mercy. In tongues unknown while donning Cheshire grins too perfect for credibility. In self adulatory contentment that the spirit is losing both battle and larger conflict. Lost in flight after struck by homing pigeons which were can't remember the address. Discovery of which shouldn't come as a surprise if it's where the heart is. Still in search thereof while tending wounds scabbed over only to be torn to bleed immediately following formation of protective keloid. Tissue designed to persevere can't go the distance let alone dry an eye. Enraged at inability to conjure up satisfactory results in a 'civilized' manner though willing counterparties are few and far between. Warm and cuddly are tricks of conveniently applied patter softening jagged truth to smooth stone with medieval grating devices emitting mind splitting drivel. Great society isn't looking so regal though that isn't really the point here. Just one link in an electric chain long since violated with haphazardly wielded bolt-cutters and flying off the mantle closed-circuit links. Symptomatic disconnect in a disjointed epoch which is too much to go into at this point but to illustrate that were I able, well received it wouldn't be. Perhaps I should say when instead. You won't like it. Promise. So by all means, dislocate your spineless vertebrae reaching for disunity under a severed flag. Define what you don't understand. Crack your stale corn. Danny don't care. He's too busy looking for the kid he's never met. The one you'd never receive.

Cereal

Slinking down aisles stacked with an eclectic amalgam of droning corpuscles tapping out some sort of rhythm which sounds less than a bit nasally though everything is muted by an unintelligible din.   Matte Play-Doh faceless sweating respiring decisions before abundant shelf space requiring action deliberative so as to obviate its usage in delusional communal context. Well, if the plot's to maintain believability anyway. Mute lambs minting jelly with swipe of magnetized plastic. Anonymously scanning barcodes off boxes. Off club cards. Off conscription numbers carved into psyches.   An accidentally tapped gallon jug puddles the tired chessboard mated with countless soles of innumerable souls and all they've traversed or trampled. Row of beans has me steaming. Cereal is turning into a real drama. Chilean plums are speaking in a rapid dialect a bit foreign to me yet somehow rescue my vision which goes from still-life to surreal upon entry to this infirmary.   A musky flavored zombie grabs convenient idiot proof plastic and mindlessly fills it with carrots before twist-tying a Russian canine task to completion. To the cabbage patch for roughage guaranteeing mundane will digest future events long past host-less expiration. Basket wheels rolling their own dope- trains glued to mechanized tracks in no order which I've discovered though I'm still sniffing around with functional actuarial substance however it seems evident higher margin locations have a more frequent schedule. What would Stepford look like in Korea? What does lost in spanglation have to say, ese? Blue eyed devil running through meandering lyric with intermittent pattern-less breaks making the whole slalom that much more difficult. As time slows to 1/8th speed. As the checkout girl has touch screen disposition plugged into a missing job though they supposedly found it somewhere in or about a sterile non-descript Palo Alto edifice specializing in animating automatons. Each neuron proceeding ever closer to clean room predetermination.   Functionality otherwise left to devices of reproductive hordes who wish not to be involved in determinations.   No sharper than watered-down gourds anyway. Undoubtedly delivering progeny into eternal impotence for however long eternity lasts which is an open-for-reward applied physics equation on which nobody's got the balls to expend any kinesthetic capacity. Questionable granting of power to control destiny is a tie that binds. A rope that hangs itself. Wonder drug of whomever is selling the wonder oil. Watery baptism though nobody catches the faith before it drowns in its own excess. Even Moses couldn't part the mouth of this river. No dam can stop its progression. And not a mob in the world can fly backwards. Destiny's child is carved in chocolate chip. Down 18 on the left. Though I guess that's how the cookie crumbles. And cities breathe putrid smoke to paint cigarette warning billboards in Crayola lung-black. Former glory now a dying hue. Victim of its own success. Burning all the way to the bank while the rest of us fry under a dime-store copy of the sun which happens to look like a whole lot of crimson nothing though shan't be discounted cuz a whole lot of nothing can still choke a goat. Lines of which are chewing the rag around laced bales in the shadow of indiscretion hidden in self induced retching of soul before consolation prizes are announced.

Jazzin' It Out Of Town

Stranglehold highway loses its grip at zero dark something. Hyped on Korean roast beast on three hours of loping REM sleep. Irreverent child breaking free of obstinately demeaning nanny without any non-native reservations but I'm reconsidering. Scrambling for cover of darkness and open road. Washing sins of the urban off noticeably crinkled skin. Racing impregnable loops of successively narrow passage navigated under lights of a city bidding fuck you while in the distance, winking moon-shadow lights paths for a cosmic greeting which on its face, is not necessarily a comfort. Un-cinching the garrote eating through the night while drinking Burma-shave in hoarse vocals channeling the report of yesterday which today rots in anachronistic purgatory. All signs wasting in potters' fields of a lost path in dying dream so nobody knows the way anymore. Hidden from view are all directions one needed, languishing with rusted tractors and retired ambition. Storied route-droppings turned prized kitsch. A different day and time-warped dead-of-color reverie. Multi-axles jockey for pole position throwing cruise control into a mad frenzy. Violent gusts smack face first as if to say go back whence you came. The winds are sometimes possessed and prone to demand conviction. They haven't caught me yet. Swooning tumbleweeds dance a dangerous game on the highway. Like the rest, even scrub will litter the atmosphere with granular history. Twinkle of brightest of stars comes to view as progressive hillside lights hindsight in flames torching the hypocrite sky- acting out my favorite scene. Let's go to war and get it over with. Digressing- could be the north star. Can't make out Orion's belt from a shot in the dark. Besides, stars lie too. Could be simple omission but begging notice of long-expired radiance seems foolish and any demonstrative expectation for same exceedingly narcissistic (redundant- yeah) and presumptuous (possibly redundant as well- consult who gives a fuck). Could just be fabled wool hiding a call to the abyss. Take a leak in desert shrub, black but for big rig snore and unheard rattles in the bush. Rising peaks beckon a heavy foot. Lids falling like anvils bumped to attention by intentionally marred asphalt. Sparse is everywhere. Thinning air turns green. Land of rising sun sends the gift west. I want a return. With it, Pandora's box illuminates the horror. It's difficult watching the evils write wicked dirges so as one might expect Boris Karloff to enter focus. A train traverses a mountain pass, long haul in tow. Landscape worth every cent the exhausting price of emission. Languid decompression gains interest but its rate has limits. Gazing at the intoxication that are screeching boxcars, I swear all I see is failing foundation buckling under the weight and unless I'm just paranoid, I'd bear witness to boulders above- shifting position. Guess I could mention something about red rocks and circling birds of prey though that might border on something politically incorrect if not carefully constructed. I failed woodshop.

Nothing Sacred

Skirting the issue while preserving obligatory silence under seal of new-age dictum of incongruous genteel interaction is nipping at my buds and taking the stalk with it. A dose by any other name tastes less sweet after the second coming. Semantic dislocations taking verse from the heart. Holding hostage dialogue which ran hull-straight into deep freezing gasps of how could you from frothing lips whispering intolerant ventriloquism through congealing marionettes. Riding a valiant steed over opaque platform of transparent foundation. Misanthropic angle is spitting ovals into square legs. Not intended for public consumption is devoured by a passing comet which fails to clean the bowl. Slipping into a new way of thinking is gripping to tried and true while repellant voices wax diluted polemic, clothing the artichoke in masticated petals leaving no alternative but for armed resistance or at least a sharpened sword from preshrunk stone-washed genes. Gaming the table with drunken mice. Chasing the bogey with an eagle-eyed view of crumbling empirical data. Lost in translocation is contrary to proven methodology so to be safe, I'm speaking in tongues and only to the deaf. Surprisingly few can read the card. Its decimals bouncing between truth is stranger than friction and moralistic high ground assessment of astigmatic movement permeating bowels of peritonitic pupils found wandering aisles of arcane murder mysteries labeled social discourse which has more than a slight hint of oxymoronic. Opening flood gates to a dry river which won't stop running its mouth off. Rustling feathers of who knows better but can't elucidate for fear of multi-grain reprisal. Leveling off the picture at a seventy three degree slant matching inconsistency of incontinent revolutionaries donning smartphones ringing utopian hymns laced with trace amounts of sundry caustic substances. Misogynistic template for world domination was trashed in favor of misandristic font though it shouldn't be a surprise as those balls have long been in their bucket regardless and they know just to where to plant the fuck me? No, fuck you pumps. A Mexican crossed the border and his back got wet. He dried off and got a job. Camel killed in freak accident perpetrated by seven year old jihadist with YouTube and an erector set who himself was then shot to reward his sacrifice. Received his seventy two though still has nary a clue as to what to do with any. Redman is lionized though scalping didn't start with Plymouth Rock. I always feel a nip in the air in early December. Yellow horde couldn't drive to save their sight. Germans are still Nazis as are the fascist Jews with dystopic delusions of grandeur commonly referred to as members of my own tribe which shutters the scaffolds. White men still can't jump or bump and rarely hold up under scrutiny. Calling a spade a spade which could be best hand or failed promise without sacrificing white knuckled conspiratorial attempts at my Atheist Yid cracker epoch. Robes folded into neat patchworks of unsuspecting parishes when defrock and deflower belongs in papal order. And in the deepest closets of the darkest hour of any hater of men is a lover of man (special reference only, gender non-specific and don't get me started on it, light loafers) for precisely the reason of affinity for the singular. Perhaps not parallel on the surface though judging books by cover or failed euphemism is thin binding. Plural can be a mobbed-up affiliation of prosthetic triviality standing in front of its own confirmation for another opinion. And sometimes sauerkraut is just a mad Bavarian though color me cynical. We'll never know until we hash it out to allow poppies their bloom. Contents combust spontaneously while regaling one-world lunacy with condescending insolence of thinly veiled when it should be laid on thick with dear antes which may tend to insult the tar on the way to truth however, for four letter words are unwelcome even with five characters. Doc and bashful have gone missing under a pile of expectation for serene-seeming, trying too hard at happy to be trusted would-be Hindus wishing to come back as Sikhs or sacred cows. And to those who've gone un-enunciated, it's only for lack of space, limited time left on the tilted axis and no concern for your feelings whatsoever. Congregation of a magnanimous pipedream sacrificed in lieu of mangling the mangrove. All who care, raise two hands and hope for the best. Shaken not stirred is call of the wild wolves howling for their own. PC is spelled incorrectly. Carlin flips his pine lid. The truth may have fallen dead off a cross or poked itself on six points which is distinction without difference. Maybe it's just stuck in fear of revelation (small case). Never to be defused until the pressure cooker melts the meat from bone and we meet with revelation (large case) or a close facsimile for those of us who believe in aria not rapture (large case).

Tombstone

Encumbered space missing a key component hasn't the jazz to make me hum. Riding the lighting into new-age blend is a wired attempt at ignoring cruel intention over wireless networks that don't seem to get together too often. Tossing out the first pitch can be a chronological advantage or a walk in the park when thrice repeated. Casting aspersions at open door policy is a closed audition. Retreating from confines of nominal space beyond time limitations is unleashing amputated limbs from bondage which seems a bit too late for a stroll on a lark or slice of caked-on deceit which doesn't hold the ruse well. Incumbent forces are entrenched in pillars of gallows pole. Short circuitry flying in the face of advanced reason is sparking invention where sterile can't bust a virile nut but excels at tripping off the breakers in white hot vapor. Entrails splayed inside four walls don't yet know their place though facial depressions belie the missing poetry of tombstone justice that could be a step in the wrong direction or simply a wide swath of incomplete fabric. Toppling despots in any way possible though the targets never suspect a thing. Wondering where the long resolution is. Where unsuspecting notes follow in seeming non-sequitur which tends to follow more than previously suspected. Resolving itself in the word. Divining rod of good intention is drawing on scratched echo and not in tune with the recumbent melody in my head which has halted progression in protest of the counter's collective assault. Sipping mother's milk though she creates quite a mew. Spanking silhouettes of former glory is seeking release however can't come to a swift conclusion. Climate is cooling at a rapid pace. No surprise if not-ideal dynamics are no surprise. Unsuspected recoil snaps to inattention though the blowback is still substantial. Putting together a narrative which doesn't tell much of a story yet under the covers is a world of unheralded emotional impact. Is a damper to escape to cowardly old world, vibrant as ever and more so in hyper-ignorant wanderings depleting youth its resource, expanding diabetic horizons to new bloat. Listing in the sea is a downhill slope to avatar existence at click and invective point. Ferocity from apparitional counterparties is failing to cash the check. Insufficient funding is sucking plentiful funds though construction is functionary of inflated neuronal self image which isn't teaching much but for colloquial implication of absolute power outage which is denying anything yet blank expression of nebulous while rainbow spectrum is within grasp not getting a grip on that which really matters. And the children rot as Tricky Dick casts a sideways smile through pockmarked reminders never to be heard from talking benches etched in blood of time never served while backs break under force of self adulatory reverence to that which deserves no bookmark and never appears to get one though red checkmarks mar patterns of failure to which none will admit. The jazz still escapes on this escapade in hyped up neutral hell. Can't believe I forgot my headphones. Lacking, so goes resolution to untethered notes that have it together far more than the composer.

Insect Cry

Gliding through absurdity as it flutters its chaotic means about masses of incoherence trying to adhere to one another creating a sticky situation. Circumambulatory emanation no longer chasing its tail as the wailing returns and keys are struck. No longer a wanted poster outside the Stepford grinds. Free floating to shimmying stars wailing outside the scope of handcuffed. Dismembered fragment of dizzying magnitude is unleashing a furious attack on stasis which smells stale. Egesting truth while concealing veracity. Ivory skin is anything but white. Demanding voices command no respect though are quick to violent retort in its absence. Lights flicker in the distance. Could be an SOS or come hither call to a siren song. Something I'd never know as I failed knot-tying and would no longer recognize the latter even at a lap of the nectar. Confounded and weary though pounding freeform certain to end somewhere though destination is confidential until premier event certain to draw no luminaries among the crowd of not any. Differing configurations dangling from the short tree are sucking the sugar from spice of lifeless hoaxes which don't find themselves humorous whatsoever. Severed appendages slipping to turf sure to return as sodden implications of road never travelled. Flattop shivering in monotonous drivel while free-birds soar into the eclipse which radiates blindness on those lacking sight. Securing a spot in history is a missing latchkey. Hoping for anything better than obscurity while hiding from demonic antagonists threading the fine strands with non-virginal silkworm extract which is nothing but a way of expressing a paradox within a carefully wrapped riddle of entropic clapboard itself built on foundations of pretzel ratiocination. Retreating to the lair above to catch lamming it riffs just to glimpse a view of the outside world before recoiling in horror back to prescribed coordinates in order for rapid adjudication or at least a speedy trial. However I've always been certain of my right to be silently ignored. Consider it exorcized. Beast within spitting bile into the face of anything affronting it is getting nowhere as everything is disrespectful. Nothing more than reflective chrome or bright stainless. Clipping my own press from previous lines which may seem to violate the stream though straight edges are difficult to draw when jutting diversions swirl in a jetty holding no affinity for intractable migrants. Impossible nightmare is playing itself out though all outward indications belie the argument. The larvae await spring. Dawning of a new spawn without a doubt to result in dubious action. Quantifiable by hail and earthquake. By sprinkling of starlight and crimson desert skies. Never by means to an end for that could be a fatal mistake. A minute late can lead to a landslide victory or a totaled failure though insurers are loathe to embrace the latter. Nobody said life was fair though the prescient at least drew a roadmap which is albeit nothing but a heap of steaming anecdotal reference and past results are no indication of future performance yet does come in handy nevertheless. Or so they told me in entomology school.

Dust In The Limb

Locked in a cocoon which could be creation of beaten senseless or failed genetic lottery. Sickened by slow-evaporating haze of miasmic shifts in weather report. Towering in once swaggering reign of feigned simulacra which fooled nobody though today binds like careful for what you wish for, regularly to result in put up or shut up with a weathered though gamecock not taken to turning the other beak. Nose to grindstone dishevels top-billing. Spitting image expectorates a doppelganger which bears little in common with outside appearances intended to throw misleading scents confounding dogs hot on the heels. Chilling effect repeats until acidic repercussion calls for voice of reason unresponsive to runway foam. Crash-landing into nod. Depositing reserves in unintelligible sonic booming in two languages, neither of which reverberates in still-life though paints an enticing abstract picture. Departure from far-away lands in distant terrain with a thud on frozen tarmac. Lying in wait is a viper with a raspy hiss brought on by self preservation or simply poor attitudinal disposition. Expanding gauntlets are lines in the sand fading in a dusty wake laid by carbureted relics which rumble past fuel injected though labor at handling rattle and hum to soften the blows. Leaving on a jet plane with no flight plan but hoping to land where I started and beat that golem with a slugger. Reverse gearing is losing traction which I suppose is a good thing though the path forgotten is surely repeated. Arching beams catch the ovoid bursts of unchecked aggression which are admittedly words stolen from where the room is really tied together though the inhabitants are not. Renders them of superior nature than atmospheric pressure would have you subscribe which may become mandatory elements of survival despite staying one step behind to preserve anonymity. Soggy chemistry is leading down a dark narrow pass to enlightenment though more aware has never been sourced out depletion rather a headstrong thorn sticking to all sides. Blowing in the wind are flapping lips of dictation taken in the heat of a capitol summer. Excessive motion followed by public release. I had no, well some, well I guess it's time to come clean about my dirt. Piano in chief has ample legs for kicked to the curb. But seriously, can you blame me? Repetitious discourse even when unspoken but in the gargled steam of sweating streets while trees overburdened with aromatic coats scramble to fly south for the winter and Winnebago warriors laud the blooming effort, incapable of standing witness to swelter in the storm. Rolling joint of hermetically sealed. Grasping at straw dogs which have outlived any form of utility. Calling out bloodhounds to find what's missing though the scent has been lost to the fates and they don't budge. Not even for penance which could be a good start at breaking from the shell. Or just pie in the eye once again and another scrap of un-chosen draft picks. DNA with no trade-in value.

Excommunicated

Gone incommunicado with the lack of intelligentsia which goes by a more appealing cryptic moniker reeking of cracked vessels on overtly obsequious mirrors. Fascination with level playing fields isn't quite engrossing as might be heard on radio free America or primetime hooks to the lead story whitewashed in blackened hearts. Hard stroke to the undercarriage is a nanny who can't punch the clock fast enough. Rattling off platitudes that few can take seriously though they make serious attempts at looking serious. Collective insomniac ignoring chromosomal imbalance is taking a tractor to the fields though will perpetually tilt off its treads. Unfriendly peaceniks have a knife to me throat in search of me lucky charms while proclaiming unity with calloused reminders of best not to vocalize in public forums. Serrated bio-degradable edge so effective as to dissolve with a faint bead of perspiring rage at the sci-fi backdrop lacking the sci to balance a full head of fi steaming forward in a progression that's something like Scandinavian death rock played backward at slow speed- revelatory to no one but conspiracy theorists who keep rapping at my door for hints at future expectations but I'm out of that business and all prognostications are null and void unless attached to signed on a dotted line in indelible ink. Racking a shotgun or three into battery while stoking the mags with your day isn't looking good is the closest to free advice I'll offer any longer. Asking for forgiveness perpetually though am unsure as to why or to whom I beg but for those trespassed in several amoral youthful perpetrations in need of remediation. Something unlikely to occur in most cases as not kept up at night over this past and present is doing best it can. Interloping upon her majesty is getting old for her and a diminishing return for us which is likely outside the scope of whatever is the field of vision here however it seemed worth mentioning. And I drip a tear over transient terrain though it doesn't matter and I don't care anymore than a child concerns himself with his security blanket. Anything additional is to invoke rights and wait for an attorney before answering questioning monkeys swinging from vines, doped on free coffee and questionable motivation. Praying for faith in Atheism could be a contradiction in terms that comes together at the tip of the spear however connection to higher powers lead to electrical issues in the thorax in addition to the blown transformer which rarely gets ahead of froth anymore. Something seemingly sad because it mostly is though dramatically less so than expectation sitting mere inches above ground. Tripping the snare time and again, phosphorescent warning signs notwithstanding. Low-brow democracy in electoral format where man has no vote and the crew is revolting. Smelling of teen spirit on the set is in need of a shower and vindication of culpability. As the dogged masses have ceased chasing rabbits and new inebriants in favor of digital enhancement that doesn't seem to have made anything better but at least my penmanship is once again legible. The elite still can't read the writing on crumbling wall yet the downtrodden feel it collapsing beneath their feet. Especially when hiding from logically inconceivable zeitgeist which is punishable by banishment to the custody of the state or excommunication by communal decree for lack of a better self-image or extraneous introspection. Whichever comes first.

Seizing Third Rail

An unsuspecting levee gives way to erstwhile languid repertoire returning from sabbatical without notice. Ruffled chop shoots nom de plumes from the sky with white-capped bottle-rockets. Slipping into a different persona seems like the easy way out though current model has been years on the production line and all reparable chinks hammered out of the armor. Would appear congruous with current state of no affairs aside from chemically charged romance with jazzed up composition. Indefinable character is boiling over with hypotheses. Down in the dumps is digging out from festering blues. Reclining diffident has taken to outspoken setting the record straight. Meditating charlatans chant novenas to paper mache pachyderms- bargain nirvana for a handful of fool's gold that will soon depart for brighter horizons sure as death which is certainly a short-order not difficult to cook up. Subscribing to off the wall notions in cahoots with Spanish flies that witness less action than once though economy of language renders it an apple to orange dynamic. Avoiding the tape because I read the papers or not but between the lines screams loud and clear. Deafening silence is infuriatingly overplayed on classic rock radio though speaks volumes when cranked to eleven yet the case is cracked and primary gaskets struggle to seal fate in manifest destiny so as not to uproot the shade of known quantity. Linear conclusions are bent axles lacking grease to keep grinding at a minimum. Elevated expectations are nothing but hot air or failed constituency. Lying in wait are bleached tigers camouflaged by chipped white paint. Manic episodes have gone straight to syndication for the big bucks though nothing but post-natal does are in sight. Lacking intestinal fortitude for much but whole-grain crass while facing uphill battle for moral supremacy is existential third rail. Delineation of intent is falling into a generational gap or perhaps just too much work as flash panoramas leave little for intuitive gymnastics. Wondering where the time went while watching grains tick towards the final rendition. A performance not to be missed is estranged from principal theme. Second act is wandering the aisles looking for a seat but standing room only is the best it can muster. Lugubrious opening is leading to a big bang though the center is a sway-back nag running as a consolation prize. Ebb tide is calling for all hands on deck. Peppering in the circle to the beat of searing heat before the game is called. Meandering the disparate which all connects despite outward appearance. It's utterly inane to believe the vagaries aren't transcendent. Watch them fall off the Bernoulli device due to the observation. Heisenberg saw it coming and died for the sin. Close scrutiny is burning the page which is plainly evident and is likely to result in swift extinguishment though for now, the waters break-in new methods to what was nothing more than a left temporal study. Now nothing less than a New Orleans flood during Mardi Gras. Daunting tale which won't retract. Not even for a fistful of beads.

Vivisecting Daydreams

Passing fresh flesh is a continuous trail of too young to chase anything but off. Writing myself out of engagement as most events end in disaster or some degree thereof. Rediscovered headstrong is wrapping its head around streams of subconsciousness with chalice of sterling instinctual settings which is a hard drive from analog inspiration lost in repetitive motive power of two digits which when multiplied don't add up to much. Not wishing to impede the outflow is avoiding bar fights by eschewing virtue of primary syllable. Asking why is absurd though moving headlong into brick walls is always a coin-flip. Subsea expeditions to depths previously unheard of leaves me in an up-word graph bordering no fences- dropping bombs on past formats still in misuse to this very day while original thought is expended after the money-shot. Rapping with nobody can be lost in unheralded transposition or perhaps just banging away at a burning bush. First born male is delivered with a chip on the shoulder of self-proclaimed first son whose death had nothing to do with Romans or any other faction meant to take the blame. A long staff is siphoning wages from mislead consensus hanging from self-fashioned slipknots. Incandescent authority is lacking transparency. Repealing any and all previous inclination to wander back into tired character is at risk of redundancy which is still a vast improvement over hackneyed attempts of fools elevated to worn genres though car chases make for better receipts. Allowing for distinction emanating like diesel emission from full of gas. Breaking wind into warpspeed collision course is a juggernaut that is at this point irretrievable framework of cinemagraphic mayhem or just a step forward with dissonant implication though smacks of sugar not previously ripe for caning. Interior dimensions grow while patience sits on the sideline in need of medical attention or at least psychiatric intervention. Mania is engulfing the entirety with necessary impetus yet draws a blank stare on occasion which can spur the stamina to beyond capacity or push the horse too hard for continuing to the next chapter. Declining invitations is getting old though fails to reach gargantuan proportions obligatory to change course. A hermit copies and pastes fatalistic what have you under the watchful eye of coed gargoyles that never stop ragging for more. Will never learn is a small head with a large ego shrinking in a cold pool of sweat. Apparently a widely held stasis though to further illuminate would cast a palling light on a black whole. Devoid of a tug to action or any shot at the full moon. Watching the wheels go 'round. Dissecting all elementary data is finding no logical solution to the vivisection. Cutting into conversation are high-grade logistics that never get anybody anywhere. Like a chimp caged in a roadside attraction which is anything but becoming. Staring down open auditions like a crack pipe, knowing fifteen minutes of fame are the best that can be asked for. Or at least that's what the voices tell me while slobbering over unwelcome revelries.

Obviated Battle Lines

Slamming multi-media with singular focus. Pregnant dialectic is breaching the trellis under watchful eyes that can't believe what they're hearing so choose mute rather than revolt. Sustained iniquities getting preferential treatment which should remain in effect as long as the warranty hasn't expired which is objective thinking under a subjective sun. Riding the rails to heartland on a thing and a prayer that hasn't much for higher power though casts a disapproving glance in my own direction. Unknown entities placing themselves in harm's way refuse to tend their wounds. Succumbing to fear of the moment or momentary lapse of treason is betraying the cause which has lost its footing in bog that seems a little slow on the uptake. Cracking a whip at convention that would have one believe seemingly disjointed is what it seems. Redirecting channels from what could have been had I left a moment sooner or the bus departed two minutes ahead of schedule is either a flat line or abundant disapproval wobbling on firm legs. Created in some image is insignificance personified. Din of chaotic rumblings would have you believe everything's under control beneath its authority. Nothing farther from the truth implicates celestial wanderlust though never believe party lines. Snuffed out in a battle of wits with witless is unlikely though small guys fall softer. Recreating a battle sequence is bloody business however suppositions need something to rely on. No stranger grips my hand though harrowing tales are repeated ad nauseam as bolts shoot from unrepentant abundance that don't have concern for individualized plight which is not necessarily pecuniary blight but a humanistic approach that lost its landing gear and circles the tower dumping fuel and jet trash on true believers who genuflect in throes of comatosed fugue. Lapping tides of warfare are taking a licking with sandpaper tongues shaving off the rough edges to no avail. Counterintuitive conceptual weave is coming undone at the worst of times though aren't they all? Genetic coding isn't programmed for societal expectation any more than man's law. Unmodified linguistics toss society and community out with the bathwater of a billion times seven divided by two arguments either steeped in battle or flat out on platitudinal scales in hostile keys. Trying to make sense of it all is to trip up unconscionable notional inconsistency while logisticians die in their sleep counting bounding sheep in complex dreamscapes which when whittled down to the grain are nothing more than base-age accusations of troubled minds incapable of rest when the wicked are plying their lecherous trade. Bobble-head dialogue is sullying attempts at whatever it is they're trying to babble though shifting winds prevail and the antics don't hold water. Boarded up intake valves lacking gross margins have stopped forward motion of the progression though it should come as no surprise given that shock value is diluted by means of flash-photography and scandalous intervals which used to take more time to disseminate though seeds have been planted and insemination is imminent where not already full speed ahead into social networks with an unmistakable reek of anti-sociopathology. Drying on vines is their day in bitingly droll spotlight. Recounting what went wrong though can't hear themselves think with overlapping squealing- diminishing capacity to know what it is they're fighting about however any fight is a good fight provided nothing gets done in the process. Songbirds are tweeting broadside into ether where they once might have simply crowed to small crowds.

Insignificant

Inconsequential protoplasmic detritus strutting as if there was a point to their existence. As if the universe will whisper a prayer while three shovels toss yesterday's hero to more apt insignificance as if Orion will loosen his belt following a gluttonous wake. As if a Cajun dirge would march during lent. An escapade into a dire mantra may get you through the day or could be a self-fulfilling prophecy. Pleading for exoneration does little when caught red-handed during proceedings. Wallowing in decalcified bone-meal which does little to reclassify the night though laying down only hurts half more than getting up- itself a risky proposition when under cold wind blowing. Practicing avoidance is another way of disconnect or closer link with someone entirely more appealing. Unleashed connection with perpetuity is set to demise at to be determined. Lacking insider information makes for a tough trade though history provides some juicy details, mostly forgotten in hallucinogenic haze of marbling beefs and melting cloaks which is multitudes better than a sure thing. In processed fat screaming from inanimate sources for a draft choice to be named later though a steady flow of tips bets on poor planning or ambition misappropriated by a narcoleptic treadmill. Serpentine expectorant spitting lifeblood in eye of the beholder which could see the beauty if not for blinded by the bite. Fanning egos are catching a warm breeze which is another way of saying one-way street if the road gets bumpy. Tomorrow may never come is scrawled in a white plume beneath Coppertone ads. Proclamations of extended life expectancy yield a hard rain. Tomorrow doesn't care. Racking all available units to extinguish flames while digging pyrotechnic holes for future combustion. Taking the bully-pulpit in plain sight to try a novel approach at remaining unheard. Speak loudly of that you plan. They could use a good laugh. Overestimation is entertainment of life won't go on. Word not worth the time it's taken to get this far. It will sail past your wildest fantasies right into her deepest abyss. Struck by eight death-knells. Near-miss renders expert opinion though close call is one cigarette away from a full pack. One eyed jack with no bouncing balls. Only security in the fact that it really doesn't matter but in the moment which isn't a nano-tick in the fur coating. That tomorrow will eventually not. And following a crocodile tear or two, the sun will cast shadows upon the dawn and the moon will glow at dusk. Rivers will mouth off to greater opportunity. And your tread won't show up in either plaster cast nor bronzed bust. Inevitability matched with reality is the spawn of Cerberus drunk on Dionysus. Someone awaits your arrival. Like a sales-force awaiting fortune of opportunity knocking the door of preparation into expanded sense of insecurity and eventually, indescribable loathing, so often well-deserved. The dirt doesn't care anymore than tomorrow. It's good for business.

Nipped Bud

Slipping towards it's darkest before the dawn while trying to maintain flooding tributaries is holding on by skin of caving toothpicks. Rewarding extra effort with a gold star but not much else. Commercial pick-me-up is whiffing its act. Drooling fingers search for familiar shelter. Intransigent gesticulation is fighting off desire to put a fork in the whole enchilada. Unretractable yawning is holding pole position though is at risk of second wind. Irretrievable lingo is hiding behind the sofa which is the last place I'd look, explaining its sex appeal. Picket lines are picking at scabs though even dissent hungers. Amiss scribbles look like censoring leaves though the gig was up at conception and even a one hand snap grab was obviated by the lack of a halter. Hard up is looking for safe harbor as was its lineage is its progeny. Batty wife syndrome was actually a product of crude wood cut-outs though some caves were thought to exist among the higher on the monkey pod. Rewritten history is at risk of retraction for an umpteenth revision which doesn't change the theme though the plot thickens like settling mortar. Rounds drop from all directions and the foxhole is crowded with Atheists. Land war in Asia risks crushing rubble into rubble. Jihad makes for good bylines though soundstages make better use of the explosive material. Mel's an anti-Semitic asshole paid by Semitic assholes to maintain that all differences aside, we can foxtrot to direct deposit in peace. Incredulity strikes a high note, devouring two Twinkies and a harlot between hits. Straight up is leaning towards horizontal marketing which would shutter the production line though IVs are easily enough replaced. Headstrong associates are muddling the scene like a lone Asian to a bell-curve. Summary execution is halted for confidential diplomatic ends for which we await a synopsis. Trivial pursuits look more like smoking guns though just a few minutes a day can pack on an inch or two. Tugging along with over laden sampans through Hong Kong harbor is picking up stragglers for a new film. Waters push and pull to take the shape of their carriage. Humanoid samplings tend to shape the conveyance around the water which doesn't much care for the hijinks according to four out of five dentists surveyed. Saccharine overload is filling holes in the script with lolling half-wits who couldn't make the cut with a straight razor. All liability has been disclaimed by management, including but not limited to legal implications of oversized beverages toppling gargantuan egos of undersized despots with more heat than they can handle without handlers but then there's always Elba. Off with their heads has naming rights to the era under direction of Lorena Bobbitt. Cockpits aren't. Slap and tickle affiliations are cracking unwise. Jocular is launching an arrestable offensive though few are taken aback anymore. Desensitization has assumed sentient command. Full Metal Jacket sits next to Barney at Blockbuster. Jaded too early is right on time. Get it straight young'un. Sometime before sleep sets in and ranting is out of the question. Before the puppets start talking and the monster under your bed materializes despite parental sermon. Notwithstanding the gore you will experience upon shuteye. The branches reaching towards you while thunder claps and rain is an undertow dragging you down without a paddle. And for god sakes, far in advance of the beating you'll take for the experience. Hopefully antecedent to any comprehension of the incomprehensible rigmarole which dead ends here in typical fatalistic fashion. Something not on the shelves at Saks Fifth Avenue though receipts are robust for those who learned too late and need a parting gift before the production goes off Broadway. And Broadway falls off the map. But sleep tight, Mrs. Lincoln. There're a few cans of Turtle Wax left.

Resurrected

Catapulted dreams winding down a forgotten trail with too much memory. Disregarding tracks in snow is a sure way to hypothermia or an un-violated pathway yet to be disgraced by latent prints which are patently destructive and lead one to cliff's edge if pondered extensively. Counting chips which are an ante I wish to pull back given my track record though nothing's doing and the sharks smell blood. Eaten alive by idiomatic deficits. Reddening welts are unresponsive to treatment however itch less than once. Was a time inconsistent logical counterbalances lost their equilibrium over such trifles. No time for skipping stones is passing a steady flow of ideas my way. None look much like a trip to promised land or even an incredulous wink and nod. Glancing up from a hole in the wall is a sparking socket which seems to lack connection to movements of cliques which is only a positive as I snap at conceptual mobs which fail to factor no consent into their cost basis, alienating the invention before chance meeting takes place at the cross-roads of tribal nature and kinder gentler view from above. Laughable on its face though it won't front the music. Predisposed to guarding what's whomever's is a peak high on its own thin air. Can't acquiesce to a heavy hand though a softer approach may prime the pump. Questionable motives are not being interrogated at present. It could be a long time coming before necessity dictates their appearance for an interview. Guarding all secrets with funambulist dialogue while huffing white-out which always seems to bless impaired auditory with a looping bass-line and unrecyclable paper sacks. The baggy and damage done are placing toll-calls on overworked lines. Stuck in a bind but no longer bound by picket sticks that serve little purpose aside from alienation of we are not alone. Inconceivable universal mass is eloping with unrepentant ne'er-do-well cooked to a crisp. A shot in abysmal daydreams only and not reality based nor suitable for any audience. I'd otherwise take all the action of the pessimistic sort which has also been referred to as factual. Of a tidal wave of flowers delivered by Eros or his henchmen. Betting on long-shots is a fool's paradise smelling of stale brew and bile. Of dead and buried though still standing for the moment which is an unrecognized foible 'cuz who wants to meet the gates with busted teeth and broken nose. Figure one would employ all available strategies to at least look presentable though the kingdom is awash in dirty floors. My death waits in an alley that will reach out and grab its prey. I'll go quietly into my own rules under Atheistic guidance. Likely an oxymoron though side of the aisle is really the determining element. Drooling at opportunities missed is getting older than me- my beard is an oxidized grey hiding a baby face which never had much chance at exposition of the latter. Last chance is placing punctuation precisely at vanity's point though leaves open possibility this too shall pass. Period.

Requiem For Vital Adjective

"i have nothing to offer anyone except my own confusion."
~kerouac

Dangerously close to tethering my ball-gag to satirical insight into what's not abject madness though remove the adjective and I may just get my first degree. Lost on a lonesome path across gila tracks seeming to flicker tongues at ray of hope infruition. Monster in the mirror is a saint in the tip cup. Screeching to a halt at conventions I rarely enjoyed if even invited. The party's too big for agoraphobia. Nonexistent vapors rise off the tar in the distance beyond red boulder construction of time and wings fluttering over stovepipes. Secreting all I feel while feeling more than I'd like to let on in any setting more formal than a roadside circus. Implying nothing but garbled messages in a burning bush. First born that should have been tossed in the stream traveling about his own perplexity decrying the last twenty as twenty short of rest in peace of mind or anywhere else for that matter. Subjected to all I allowed is survivor's guilt or ennui in a Cobain sort of take on Descartes. Listless inertia is getting nowhere. A boxcar on a hill rattling as the coyotes howl revelries to freedom from the most oppressive as long as anonymity is maintained which seems to be the crux of the ambiguity. Of the argument in favor of running to destination unknown. Not missing a minefield by choice as adversity builds character in theory though nobody's checked in with me lately. In a roundabout way is a cul-de-sac with a square end concealing gilded twists of faith which diminishes all life plans towards spiritual enlightenment in an institutional manner if not compelled by a Thorazine drip backed by Lithium cocktail to wash it all down. Interloping on what isn't mine to trespass though receiving no condemnation finally has me in a comfort zone some miles from area 51 though the cosmic alien dust could travel which would explain much but why waste my time when I could be rubbing my lucky charms which haven't picked a winner in at least a decade. Watching tumbleweed wink as it sails by in a tornado vortex- dry heat which beats the fuck out of humid freeze. I have a meeting planned with my philosophy somewhere near the dreadlocked Haight. Hoping to escape the hippies unscathed is simply foolish but life's a fool's game and stressing it won't help a damn thing. Of course I'll never take the easy road so I'll just wind the curves posting teardrops here on your eyes.

Institutional

A round thrashing is overdue though nobody has required machinery. Shenanigans perpetrated by elected are responsibility of slithery constituencies entrusted by ignorance with managing affairs of state which don't seem to have much anything to do with so-related workings worth enunciation. Frequented pubs are drunk and disorderly though far easier to digest than fermented bullshit. Digging for a point to the exercise is examining inanity from a whole new perspective or perhaps not. Swinging from questionable integrity worn down to threadbare. Scanning future passings which may seem nice from afar but are most definitely far from nice which likely deserves explicatory substance that won't be found anywhere here but between the weary lines. Releasing spirited arguments is losing its verve. On the last leg of a remarkable journey would be a nice epigraph though I'm looking to cook-off the primers. Besides being a delusionary reverie I'd prefer to remain as such, dusted off in front of a crowd is most definitely not in my first will, let alone last. Testimonial arguments are fairly convincing though I haven't confidence in the ashen implications of my departed soul. Clearly putting cart before horse but sometimes even a stallion needs a break, let alone paradoxically thankful soon-to-be adhesive. Planning ahead never seems to come to a boil though infected tissue is more noticeable when rendered illegal. Solid start and stopping point though I shan't spare succeeding space its proper dioxide. Running on faith disavows weak knees. Walking would do if the exalted is due. Weekly genuflection doesn't go so far as to callous spiteful skin, ergo by no measure can demonic bats free their sin. Overly absorbed with hereafter isn't so much the game changer which might be deemed requisite, rather an academic study of illiteracy that reads its way onto the stage with good reason. A certain glimpse into maybe-land which can't make up its mind. Catching prevailing winds of terms and conditions though understanding foundation is tempting futility. Some may say vanity though I'm too humble to admit acting in concert. Decimating preconceived notions which may have some veracity however nothing is to be discovered in the blast-zone. Taking repose in smoking 'em 'cuz I got 'em is less relaxing with occluded vessels. Arguably could be a decent rationale for cessation though cessation takes care of itself, doing so often and seeming to appreciate the work. Not to mention- reasoned can be overrated. Like an author proving his net worth is far less than his net receipts. A governing mass of tremors collecting supporting documents for the Trojan horse they'll undoubtedly let through the gates. If only I had enough staying power, perhaps I'd experience the climax and watch the zebra charlatans fry like Louisiana catfish.

Extraneous Scenes

Surrounded by fossils and skeletons, feeling secret shuddering of decalcified holographic snapshots of an autobiographical nature. Picture perfect display of the greatest blemish. The grandest cruelty. Flame or turf awaiting new arrivals with each birth keeping meticulous records for internal audits. The trees outside know my name and have for decades of etched initials in forgiving bark. Almost as if the eucalyptus beg a guestbook signature. Sputtering age is striving to be saved from linear sterility. Bouncing off double entendre like a hyped racquetball but it's only a diversionary tactic. Seeking a voice where once rasps ejaculated venom into karmic write-off. Exacting revenge for transgressions of faint echo is peeling the onion with too sharp an edge. Nonetheless, the thoughts cross my mind. No escape exists for existential prison but punishment from singularly unforgiving hanging judge found in scrambled superego on judgment day which is every. Stepping forward is two steps behind the time and won't submit to the dotted line. Petrifying course of events is a lifetime in the making or an empty chamber filled. Discourse intended for the many pulpits is drowned by committee of none. Not disturbing is being left out of the crowd. Futility bonded by single purpose that not one can express satisfactorily or even provide mild amusement. Derided deranged and hoping for a way out before the final inning though all roads lead home. Some just fight Nazca ovals. Can't believe a fucking thing anyone says is axiomatic though is as of yet, not cliché, perhaps due to its graphic nature which should be the exact reason it's recognized as a life lesson every bit the gravity of don't run with scissors. Dreaming peripatetic without moving a muscle. Running circles in a rectangular hallway. Noticing bits of missing elements which could be indications of premature dementia or more likely late onset psychosis tripped up on stress disorders and faulty wiring which occasionally goes up in smoke with purple haze hanging over my digs and the million syllables conceptualized and forever gifted the winds in the course of a single day. Is one brick shy of a full pallet an imperfect fence or flawless replication of conditional lucidity? Rhetorical questions lose appeal after rhetoric is deemed grandstanding in the cheap seats. But the bones are strewn so all may face the future via a porthole to the past while trying to avoid eye contact. Staring into its black heart, I deliver a challenge. So far the bus hasn't come. No close calls with lightning or any gods with a sense of humor though the latter is a question of whether they're laughing with me or at me. And in the end, it's an un-editable wrap. Likely a tortilla contraption in a fast food robe soon to litter the streets with no worries- it'll all be over soon enough. Presaging the obvious with boldness of world explorer. Yet in the end. The end. And but for the opening sequence, nothing else matters.

Reincarnation

Shattered faith in a system which has gone on to crushing skulls into sour candy. Emotional upheavals aside is rationalization of defensive maneuvers in face of offensive commentary from the mouths of capricious infantile whole. Nowhere to conceal palpable rage is twitching cockles of history's manifestation. Legging into the subject lightly is treading casually with heavy steps. Spurring the moment into a mangled collection of mind orgies is an aviary of distinctly guano aftertaste. Flavor of the day is revolution for sake of revolution which run in cycles though few know how to pedal. Hand on the back is either comfort or downward pressure on still not up to speed. Crash landing on a planet with unforgiving asphalt is nadir of spirit or trampoline. Dopamine anti-gravitational flip or quadra-pod extermination. As they see fit though they are a vastly overrated entity with far reaching tentacles designed to divide and conquer via offerings of salvation from all maladies regardless of clashing reference points or simply incredulously anointed cream deposited atop dregs. Sullen faces at the bar are lighter shades of death. Sometime in descent's barebones timepiece is a secret truth though to reveal it might complicate the clock's rooster cackles. Stumbling blocks placed with masonry precision are pillars of internalized loathing or stepping stones to another dimension. Total recall, an abuse of process or perhaps inventor thereof, mistakenly referred to as a gift which dangles a eulogy off rafters. Striking beauty is an interesting cover story for an evening get-off though breakfast can't come too soon if at all. Beneath the implication is a debate for under cones of silence. Nobody hears a fucking thing anyway, so why bother perfecting the technology? Perfect, as redundantly disseminated is inseminated with flawed character. Development stunted with a slap on the ass only stings more as memory centers pump iron, leaving more space for misdirects which are plentiful and abundant while indigenous struggle for a mackerel in a sardine can only to bleed off tin cuts. Lying in wait for my soul is my dagger. Is my bull barrel, red and black nicotine carton and hormonal milk. Maturation stunted by gene and heavy hand- inexorable move forward at the speed of dopamine while bellies expand practicing modern warfare from a leather sofa. Remainder is what remains. Is fractional. Factual, but rarely true. Jagged tors dotting unforeseen landscape. Salvageable journey only when unanticipated is presaged with malice of forethought that can be the only way out of the jam though can jade the best diamond in volcanic optimism. Rough riders pull out before climactic ends flood lifeblood into toothy grins. Always looking for new passengers on the flooding ship. On the burning seas. Rollicking nausea inducing catastrophes like two trains departing from otherworldly stations at the same rate a half hour apart, intending to pass in the night only to go bump. Conductors die too. Usually first. Victims of a world which refuses the bends on behalf of narcissus. Behind every corner is a new-age rice-cake to recreate the scene while staring into the very same placid pond. Conveniently after the fact. Always after the fact. I squashed a snail today. Wonder who it was.

No Happy Endings

Wondering whether sleeping on goose-down is a swan song or tar blessing in feathered disguise. Watching the clock as hands strike midnight glass like pestilent gnats girded for their station in the unforgiving expanse of freak occurrence. Driving home the point with an inch thick brad in concrete is tempting contemplation. Unstable footing is paranoia or they're still out to get me which are in no way exclusive of one another. Knowing the enemy is only half the mandate. Carnal information is price of admission. Striking out so often as to miss the roster. Riding the dark horse through hallways while seemingly invisible. Pulling from flame-out is either Nietzsche from the grave or final dejection sending you to neighboring plot. White rabbits are never caught though change spots like chameleons to blot their own reflection in post-modern art which is harder and harder to cop. Unacceptable pupils are blinded by massing grey clouds over mono-tonal beige accusers, deaf to the thunderous crack. A ticket to ride is a stranger on the road. Blood in the seat is sweat of guilt laced with weakened steel shavings. An existential nightmare is nothing but everything. Continuing examination of testing methodology is back breaking call of the wild. Barking not up to expectations until the tree is bare. Grander visions give way to motion of thousands of ghosts up from the tube on a World Trade Center seven am pilgrimage. Sea of some aren't any longer imbedded with just arriving. Dripping fucking new guy without letters to cover the scratched marks. Etched calls to anarchy in pinstripe puking at sight of hitherto unknown though something more than Bushmills painted alphabet city which more spoke my language however some secrets are best kept in mixed company. Cog in wheel of capital appreciation is no longer lubed on the idea though to each his own. Easy to present the ether when in possession. Something to which I'll incriminate myself despite setbacks to be delineated or those already revealed under separate cover. Wishing it were all different however starlings don't fly straight more than swarming wasps. Fraught with deteriorating infrastructure transcendent of highway to man is classless proposition but some solicitations are best made conspicuously in well lit areas. Recovering rage-aholic claims quitting is easy for the fourth time this week. Broken glass are wasted moments forever in hock. There is no happy ending in confounded. Brody calls out serial killer while I'm trying to keep the peace. Truces generally short-lived while angels circle the wagons and their antipodes don't care. While injecting the epoch with unfilled scripts and stepped-on scripture. Flock led to slaughter in a real jam. Suicidal sure as ghoulish moon-glow on the heart of darkness. Death of a nation certain as all the young dudes. Footnotes.

Mislabeled

Disenfranchised to the point of disinherited is calling foul though technical in nature still swallows some birds. Stellar performances mask debunked narrative. Wrapped in a shroud of secrecy in a unspecified location, admittedly not hard to find. Preferential is no incoming haze to cloud the moment with unconscionable optimism of predictably short duration. Seemingly at no risk of insurrection though always on guard. Peripheral yellow byproducts are casting a sidelong glance at the man behind the ink. Employing excessive trickery in jingo is a nice segue when what's next is undefined. Requiring yield of contextual foundation might precurse premature aging or bone crushing attention to detail. Heed is a forgotten quantity lost in flash panorama lost to the nanosecond. Exaltation is difficult to come by with high handicap. Un-replaced divots are a road to perdition or bad etiquette. Or perhaps just salt in the womb. Alone but for a Mingus riff to get the system moving towards rejected finalist. Fat on word and sugar though not necessarily happier which is contraindicated however labeling isn't always clear. Disinfecting glassware made in China though the stink won't rub off. Wiping the notes from chalkboards so as not to let the next class off with an open book which is admittedly gratuitous given probability of imminent social network failure muddying the text. Seeking free bird finding caged beast. Indescribable circumstances have deposited me at all points I'm not. Wont to wanderlust in lust of everywhere I've wandered though spit-up is a neon arrow pointed down the wrong end of a one way barrel. Lust fades like a tip of flaming spear with only cleanup work and conflagratory party burning tapes which are now melted motherboards, few of which can account for the whereabouts of offspring yet birthright is so very incorrect that ad-hoc panels now debate rules of engagement. Trying to make sense of nonsensical in direct opposition to philosophical being is scratching its head, dejected. Seeking a path to enlightenment but lacking in bread crumbs or a service station. Sucking the second hand and afterthought seatbelts recline. No helmet law is laughing at the checkpoints which have no rational point but leave it up to government. Expected funding is extortion or a bully pulpit however the lines are blurred and look too relative for nuptials anywhere but Kentucky. Blue grass is nothing I've yet smoked yet at times I would have jumped from that bridge if my friends were doing it too. A great oblivion is the realm of affection. Visiting gusts spirit wounded pride in aerosol cert. All that's left now is a final tear from all I've ever known. Simple enough on the face though even a good bluff can fall out from under you if unchecked. Racking the eight balls for a family reunion in the cabbage patch. Crying over spilled milk 'cuz otherwise I'd be laughing and that tends to violate my aesthetic though may get me thrown back in the will.

Ism

Reviewing recent attempts at character assassination concludes with revelatory marks in phosphorescent glow stretching from here to eternal omission from official report which is erecting an unstable alibi. Inhuman response to questions posed is carrying on the masquerade. A gala can be a real ball or nothing more than a self-perpetuating ode to maudlin escapades. Lambasting those who would attempt to poison the journey with utopian outcry from outlandish turf is flexing unarticulated joints to breaking point. Seven steps beyond atrophy is five shy apparently, though can't see the handbill through burning bush to make out the sex. Languid inclinations are recumbent opportunities regaling in no preparation. No-show job seeks motivated individual to collect a paycheck. Some college preferred though qualified persons shall be considered based on demerits which cuts a glacial chasm for error. Salary commensurate with inexperience. Inorganic hoaxes are taking face of kind and gentle- smashing ionic viability into a juicer to separate grease from pencil. Complete lack of metered resonance is a guaranteed trip to the great round file in the sky though rumor has it new blood is thirsting for more unmolested plasma. How can a world chock full of fruits and nuts fare any better than historical milestones- themselves lionized without aid of rapid dissemination though likely no better than syndicated broadcast? Recalcitrant upsurge is changing the face of the map again and thinks it's trying a new approach which demands blind faith in hot air. Obstinate geese are sullying attempts for departure though the engines run fine when spitting synthetic gruel. A long time coming is something beyond reasonable scope of genetic failure. Level playing field was leveled with a tipsy gauge. Darwinian hyperbole is slower moving than the graph suggests. Distorted timeframes in a funhouse pagoda wreaking havoc on tangential issue. Instant karma usurped by instant gratification which when all votes are tallied, renders a sullen woeful box stuffed to the frills satisfying no one. Realizing remember the source is truism for some ism I can't pronounce opens a vein I wished not to puncture. If ninety percent are assholes, why bother looking at hindsight unless one adheres to zeitgeist in skinny jeans Ed Hardy get-up? Notwithstanding blood on so-called peaceful palms which pay alms for a six day warranty while believers hum psalms from pierced crib sheets on torn mattresses. Spit on the gravestone is honest reflection- better than nystagmic redaction. There is no winning- only new persona lost to underground if they can catch me.

Calling Fowl

Camouflaged duck-blind types have drawn me into their quarters. Lacking alternative sources of remediation though entering with all due lack of caution so as not to break with tradition. Capitulating to reality is a barred door and untethered keystroke. Sad, but reverie is disappointment. Shadow of a doubt casts a dubious smile at cynical observations though don't get me started no matter how enticing the sentiment. Missing internal monologue is spew on a word processor. Trapped in void which is lifting me to new heights while promising to drop me like a sack of expired refills. Tending to get off the beaten track is actually a confluence of parallel events in congruent format. Forgotten art of intuition is unsalvageable chunk of road. There is no redeemable value to discarded vessels. Disappointing results stem from weak strategy or perhaps a drunken insect. Asserting all available allegations though keeping tight lipped about details. Let 'em theorize themselves. Enlightenment of one's own conclusions is rarely if ever an elective. Dogmatic misrepresentations interspersed with fundamental necessity are throwing so much red ink not even Rorschach can read the finger paint on the wall. Indefinable weaknesses are failing the levees though the runoff never ceases. Creasing the slacks where the wrinkles are taught can be a foolhardy play on words or a bad trip to the dry-cleaners from which nothing is learned. Expanding the scope beyond to conceptual planes is a giant leap off the beaten path but no great shakes for mankind. They walked on the moon though the dialogue is being called into question. Good tactic to throw us off the scent but more than a bit of overkill for the public at large. A never ending flood of afterbirth. Ever-increasing expansive girth offset by sharp rib cages though the grand balance is out of whack with Newton's third law and is under investigation by lesser beings with a penchant for useless trivia which happens to be truly fascinating. War of accumulation is doctrinal religion-state vapor which isn't aptly carbureted- fails to adjust mixture for addition of fresh air rather than depletion of the resource which may all sound oxymoronic as it is admittedly so at first glance. Second too but black light isn't shining on nothing so it must be a something lost there in them quills. Hard to come by are legitimate arguments. Simple are viral polemics broadsiding innocent bystanders with a special blend of course invective, all of which says the same thing though is worthy of redundant explication otherwise what purpose serves the term? Figure it out on your own as I'm too busy clipping my nails and wondering what vivid acts this fowl bunker is actually designed for.

Hitchhiking Under The Silvery Moon

Grinding to a short halting soprano is throwing the band out of tune or is it the other way around? Crises piling atop one another in a stack of hefty straws. Lasting forever or not a minute is getting old. Bent hypotheses can't get their stories straight. Passing a phantom menacing schoolchildren without hysterics over apparitional sighting which could get me locked up or just sent to detention. My old friend awaits recompense for truancy. Not fucking likely is underused in modern diction. Over my flattened yoga mat is more apt to be heard around these parts whose sum total is multitudes more irksome on a per capita basis than inhabitant count in latest census. Crapping over convention is certainly no way to win friends though at least removes the plated shroud and store-bought trophies. Cratered by fantastical notions of great human value is an I told you so in physical manifestation. Emotionally overbearing though antipodal alternative seems to be taking form of unyielding dichotomous dedication. Any attempt to interrupt imbalance is sent for a walking cane though not all conditions are so tilted. Capricious corners with promises of sharp edges or gentle curves don't drop their veils until too late to matter so it seems best to leave it to the fates or assume complete liability. Legal animosity awaits the latter though it remains unclear as to for what it doesn't lurk. A lawyer in every pot and I forget the rest. Missing idiomatic punctuation is no reason to exclude one from the meeting however it does call into question absent referential nuance. A light hint of mtv cribs in the background is wondering where to has gone the radio star. Have a beer in the garden and smile for the cameras. Parlor tricks rejoice at administrative calling after so many years out of work. Spikes driven through trunked up occupation though it's a corporate issue, therefore requiring no apologies and as for the workers, well they should have known better. Anything more is nothing but brevity between tranquil achievement and chaos of broken rungs. Silver spoon naiveté hopes for communal ground tofu. The tipsy ladder's holding on like Pisa. At least for now. Stress fractures are apparent. The termites have been gnawing at the subject (or object - whatever works) for generations and seem to have the upper wing occupied. Gnats in the cellar are inhaled in volume approaching straight pipes on a pan-head. Which is to say an unmuffled motorcycle in your blue-tooth. Inferring of course a potentially actionable tort as trivial pursuits lose transmission and resultant pileup of no-reply happy faces and other assorted farcical avatars causes extreme emotional distress to the party on the other line who takes to the high beam after the gym, dropping into the howling river, drowning in full view of the ferryman who couldn't care less at his wages. One might suspect a baritone should accompany the lyric though he was involved in a bicycle accident forever altering pitch. A fastball down the middle would do the same thing though I hear it's only a matter of time before baseball is banned for misogynistic tendencies or the possibility somebody might actually take a shot where it counts. All classified documents congealing in a pool beneath the scattered remnants of forgotten doctrine. In direct point of gathering nothings programmed to no longer concern themselves with self determination as it's that much easier to just acquiesce to the condensed version in high octaves, so why waste time or additional ejaculatory resonance? Maybe we are just jerking off.

Inhumane

Establishing ground rules for aerial combat while manning a missile launcher on a warship. Unleashing a hail of gunfire in the direction of full stream ahead which is by all accounts an optimistic assessment. Tracking efficiency with a sharp eye and sharper slap to pocked face. Allowances for error have been reduced to nil. All hands in all pockets on all decks in every field of battle yet none have been officially cordoned off. Broader intelligentsia has narrow-mind dysmorphic disorder. Lacking original thought or even a refreshing inkling. Sticking to chaos for a better world view. Accuracy in accounting is tallying up votes but it appears a landslide victory for it can't get any worse. Decline of civilization is oft repeated though never seems permanent. Reversion to mean is an unkind predicate for soft underbellies. Humane inclinations have no place in incendiaries as it's hard to charge the hearts of men with anything but a stoked chamber. Bodies pile atop the solution which doesn't seem to match the proof which would have to be driving highway 151 for any credibility whatsoever. Knocking down doors with a ram and rooster. Battering submission until the quill is sheathed. Opinion has lost its say in things. Under the covers, a sparrow tweets nothings and all I can do is but type despite that the sugar is always deathly sweet which is no concern of mine as I've never bought the con from the start. Instead retreating to whatever island might seem inviting though excommunicated rapidly if all goes according to plan until final adjudication locks me in with a party of one I can barely tolerate though admittedly a vast improvement over other options. Recalibrating the mechanism to accept one hand over the other. Shooting canons to Olympus though the image has already been captured and exposed. Buried under the weight of rabid road kill which smells of rotting lyric is fat drunk and stupid, son. No way to go through life is missing the fourth dimension. Flat on a plane with gravity expressed in meaningless dialectic which obviates itself in mutually assured obstruction. Rhetorical antimatter not worth the stuff they're snorting. So why stick with huffing glue when fucking them on the page is so much more endearing and seemingly unusual though with world explorer I'll never be confused? Spitting fire is a dragon in a lair coughing up the last of his, which could be before I hit send or maybe three decades from now, however I prefer spewing bile rather than threatening myself.

All Over And Black

Recollection of preceding events harping irrefutable evidence which is no more appealing when looking ass first. Speculating as to what could have or should have transpired is breathing its last breath which is a flat-out lie not even I can buy. Unaffordable continuation of failed enterprise is moderately less costly than termination of the process yet the antecedent is nevertheless a check too dear to sign and the descendant is out of the question. Something of a quagmire likely short of crisis however could be dilemma depending on parallax of optical enhancement. Walking nine steps heal to doe and returning is drunk on its own exhaust, perhaps explaining return to resting place of cadavers flipping in boxes they never checked in the booth. Scouring all crevices for a single piece of newsworthy scroll while shielding my eyes from train wrecks has left nothing but human interest stories, none of which can hold attention let alone a plant a flag at half staff. Skipping stones on a parted sea is failing to ignite any sparks though I've been told to hush so as not to alert pharaohs or revenue agents. Apparently trust in the latter has been lost wherever it was apparently once found before a sandstorm or meteoric collision. Digressing to matters of substantially more impact would be a nice diversion if only my attention wasn't otherwise preoccupied. Expansive cask of talking head extract presents without utility but wants a belt nonetheless. No way to extricate from yesterday if today is to be believed. Galloping to range in my mind begins with palominos and Stetsons trailing off to Burma-shave and skating waitress. Jukeboxes scratching and hissing what digital has unblemished to Satan's delight. Closer to the fire is each crack of the binary blip. Well-oiled machinery is seeking change but all I can rustle is a scrawled poem of a bleeding heart. Chasing windmills that were destroyed by deliberate magma. Never seeming to catch-on until everything's called off. Battery life depends upon the size of the force. Compelling inaction is careening off the walls. Is somebody watching? Wonder what that pays? Can't find the next riff in a jazz bar is switching to twelve bars which is a declination to what was which wasn't enough to hold a scale past simple weigh-in. Event calendar is infected with completed tasks. Forward looking is on a familiar path. A series of redundancies but I never claimed interwoven disparity in the fabric. Segregated ideology has been subjected to integration due to lack of space. Stragglers remain untouched. Veterans no longer expected to put in work standing on the corner watching negotiations. Interfering with surreal landscape which has passed them by in a hail of beat-ins and beat-downs and beat writers and the scuffmarks on their ragged shoes. One day tomorrow won't come.

Conspicuous And Notorious Use

Crosshairs with limited scope trained on my torso though don't have a clear read. Aimed to trip me up on some jagged wire infused with inconceivably complex small print that even the lawyers refuse to read. Stealing away in attempt to negate trepidation has so far proved unsuccessful. Reorganizing to a longer term agenda is aspiring to head of the class though even slippery pigs tire of the rat race. An entirely unwelcome event is a piece of junk mail with a toothless grin. Wandering from thought to tortuous thought is mulling about though refuses trespass warnings. Loitering in open and notorious fashion can be means of gaining ownership or perfunctory stop and frisk. Can't supply all data requested is means for cessation of contractual obligation. Fighting tooth and chipped nail for my kill. Hiding in clear sight so as not to arouse suspicion. Burning flesh on a stake in wicked river gulch just to test the theory. Eating seared roaches to test nutritional content but that's a gooey subject. Animated androids running from one nowhere to another all in search of something that's nothing while wondering what happened and where'd the time take their wives who they expected either to divorce anyway or were soon themselves to be offloaded. Rationalization of fear is patently misguided for genetics need not be reasoned to lowest common denominator. Contemplating futile tirades to get my point across though that might indicate some psychiatric subscriptions which shan't be prescribed on this scratch pad. Defer to higher sources but I've yet to find one more willing to enunciate sin so why bother seeking furtherance of loathing shadows breaking through cracks in glass? Pipes are white-hot with no sleep in sight. Still seeking a better picture on the prize though the points are sticking through concealing bush, never revealing a clean sight picture. Brazilian martial artists are sculpting a new sport though it seems that's old now and likely could be inverted if properly formatted. Dramatic entrances make for melodramatic intermissions which can be subject to watered down interlude or smashed dead soldiers. Looking instead for anticlimactic exit which sounds like an easy drive fails a blood test. Haphazard methodology skews results though usually accounts for discrepancies by cutting the class size in two and disregarding the balance which rises or falls forty percent above or below the mean which is a nasty curve to fathom but not onerous outside the confines of sign below the invisible ink. Tightly connected separation is breaking bonds in a dead heat smelling of conjoined coeds. Something worthy of shooting down, smelling all night blooming jasmine and sunflowers on a rainy day. It's only June. The reindeer are still gassing up. Small print is still after me, plentiful paranoia notwithstanding.

Munchkins And Broken Pipes

Banana brick road munchkin caravan assaulted by winged apes with no respect for tribal boundaries. Crossing the yard with seeming impunity as the convicts stare in wonder. An incomplete byline is difficult to overcome with so many naysayers about. A horse whinnies in the paddock which is breaking news and it appears holes permeate uncredible venues. Another county heard from denies easy way out while an emotional outpouring spills onto the circular town square. Expectation of higher court verdict is a grand-slam though the ball's still up in the air and elevated ambition falls harder than feather despite all physics to the contrary. Abandoning previous vocation for a broken water pipe. Rocking to rolling bass tracks looping through frontal lobes. To the best of my knowledge, unpierced though lost consciousness is a sure way to deviant practical jokes. Insidious invasion of unknown quantity delivering a knockout blow while propping eyes until arid and focused. Burgess is called in for a séance, seeking redemption for a fee. Saharan sand dune evaporates in a god's breath revealing not Atlantis but potentially a code to evolutionary misstep which has two left feet giving any point on the circumference a fair shot. Gathering steam from a ho-hum start to a yarn which has no preconceived anticipations is beginning to catch a tug on the line though something's not straight. Laughing hysterically in one's own embrace is a good quality for amateur hunter seeking a dark continent majestic beast as the hyenas pitch howling joy while betting on the winner. Purgatorial predigested bone-meal isn't buried but spread as mulch for the devil's music playing on a Wurlitzer near you today. Stepping right up to the counter of malodorous rancid pork filling up seats self-dedicated to myself upon my arrival whenever the case may be brought before my own discretion which is indeed a bit loud for the subsequent endeavor. No NWA to fuck the police but I hum a few bars under my breath before getting the runs and cleaning myself of the situation in a steaming booth nearby. Near-miss theatrics don't sound any brighter the second time, so I'll leave 'em at once. Just know it bears repeating so the latter shouldn't be taken as a manufacturer's warranty, just something like an anecdotal hypothesis. Where will the wheel stop? Where will the axle break? Betrothed interstates may lose collective moniker or just split custody once secession succeeds- sometime before the checks are useless. Internationally recognized chronicler is required reading from crayon to tassel. Is telling a story though in keeping up with the Jones' toddlers, doing so on an ether clock so hold on tight and pay close attention. The instructions will not be reposted but a treasure hunt may uncover a few clues if you put your eggs in the right basket. In the end, will I be early again and catch the train going down on ascending tracks or shall I stand at the front with forged weapon, caustic inkwell and prescription bottle? Or will I just read between the blotted subtitles like everybody else who likes having their asses wiped? Maybe I just get high with the apes if we're going backwards anyway.

Clique Away

Scribbling bombs with letters rearranged to match unruly behavior. Waxing invective on an unsuspecting public though efficacy is open for debate. Asking too many questions is a high desert burial or required reading. Compartmentalized secular cliques inexorably fight for inconsequential responses which typically end up denying the broken evening its shadow glow. Self imposed isolation is either sad and lonely or survival necessity. Scrapping previous drive to another land due to electronic elements shooting off their mouths. Laying down controversial line in the band is tooting its own horn to suicidal voices turning their attention outward. Collapsing stock price is holding back the reveries though attention to trifles is a pursuit terminated for public safety. Unavoidable truths are omitting vital details but some things are better kept locked in bulging trunks. Pandora's box is visited regularly, unleashing all new plagues with each breach of the deceptive golden locks. Making every attempt to spread toxic seed far and wide, displacing internalized debate that can't be illuminated in this forum or before women children and modern man. On a crash course with a mania bordering on lunacy though to call it insane would be premature and likely a bit exaggerative. Dumping on as many feet as I can find in the long mile. Not winning much good-will though I can't use the write-off anymore anyway. Losing no sleep over missing sheep but ancillary lightning strikes sweat bullets in vivid Technicolor depictive of exploding gourds. Picked straight from the vine and now just a bit bent. Under cover of darkness within the unwrinkled silhouette of sunshine. Capping an uncontrolled plume with more fuel for fire in the theater which nobody calls for fear of arrested development or slander. Circular logic run to absurd conclusion dying in a collision with itself at the starting line where it was supposed to end and actually did though all bets were called off out of respect to the victims who perpetrated the incident. Precipitating charred retaliations is a worthy goal or not worth the trouble. My calendar's full of open dates- leaves mood to balance options on a larger scale now that the authorities have weighed in.

Hoping with all due respect to myself to incite a riot among anarchists without a cause which opens the door for nihilistic catcalls. An outcall service is placing ads on exoskeletal scaffolds holding disintegration in check though can't take any credit for purchasing perturbed green jewels from life's general store. Offering a good deal on agonizing trinkets that prick one's existence to a series of unimportant stresses while meteors prepare to fall upon our souls. Rearranging to the best of capacity though not sure anybody will notice the difference or make a distinct observation which could be product of my own faulty rationale. Then again, I could enclose diagrams but have enough trouble erecting the machine, let alone following directions.

Quadrophenia

Cast out to the deep waters far too soon to recognize hooks for their barbs. Lacking internal fortitude to withstand another corner with gum on the nose. Fitting into a crowd with ill fitting garb is really an outside looking in proposition as is for most individuals placed in compromised positions of self determination conforming to broad regulation of unconvincingly unique peer group first chance it gets. Singular determination gathers for a council meeting weekly. Initial insecurity is closed caption before chance to spread its leaves or simply a doleful but accurate segue into the next act. Familiarity breeds clarity which is precursor to accurate world view in preemptively scathed ovals. Denying ancient truths is doing journeyman work though the sham can only hold so much water. Diligently attempting solidarity is compromised value or begging a place on the hierarchal map. Roads littered with inconsistent behavior roll on two wheels for a rumble between internal enemies 'cuz everybody loves a good fight or as good as it gets in absence thereof. Distracting attentiveness from big picture which seems so small when years have yet to add to sagging pouches before violating disunion rules with medical remediation efforts. Compromised ethics can't agree on nature of concrete intuition. Nothing short of sad is childhood lost before firm footing established. Can't get it straight no matter how many rulers have been broken in the process. Accounting for human misdeed is rightly purview of already lost to abyss of life beyond golden years which are flights of fancy that don't like being compared with blue hair that hasn't been purposefully dyed. Watching swallow of foreign tongue after misinterpreted exchange is highly effective expectorant. The golden fraud commands an army of hero worship yet to see the full document. Requisite chill is on vacation with no firm return date. Incessant preoccupation with internalized fashion debate is hopping for bells and a few jingling squares unworthy of the cause as it were. Unpleasing cinematography is panning out to catch the panorama and the smog is choking. No home for the dejected is a roof over a dismembered torso or embrace which shall never again rock the cradle to sweet dreams. Long-cut trenchcoat conceals rage of a thousand raptors interrupted at mealtime. Easy way out is launched into another song- a dirge of remorseful expression that quickly absolves its sin with a bite of a crust-less finger sandwich. Lessons not learned early may just allow for open and unfettered access though new pricing plans have made it inaccessible to most. Freedom grins with a final tear as the cliff is jumped. Antidotal ointment has been squeezed from bottom up stolen by nefarious forces destined for greatness or at least a shot that rings in the next step in the march of adherence to reigning love memorialized with a signature on a disappearing vow. Eternity is the time it takes for a goose to struggle to whole after partner is shot down like inane doctrine. Is fallacy of youth gone mad in a madder pool that can't wash the genes their inherency. Intermezzo between current wardrobe and that of been there done that and you can shove it in the queen's necklace. God save her children.

Planning Inevitable

Bucket list having trouble writing over broken bones and stained gypsum. Looks more like a paper sieve unable to hold its water. Tarred rap sheet is feathered with delicate wings unable to perform flights of fancy or other aerial maneuvers without a net though the interspersed catchalls appear tired so safety lines are strung between word pairs dangling participles from up high. Busted but not broke is still in need of repair. Clichéd countermeasures are trapped in a web that stings from outer-space while shadows of doubt are coming into the limelight. Undeveloped lands are up for auction though nobody holds title. Belt lost to new champ is utter defeat or potentially energetic fall from mountain tops and kinetic snapping lenses. Unabated daydreams are interfering with upside-down goals scored while the filthy sandman catches some a few winks. Unsure what should be considered positive ambition is draining lifeblood onto a blank page of mute expression. Crossed-out items are either accomplished or failed when hashed with red ink. Written word twisted in knots is learning to sail above the mass without instruction of higher power but who's to say? Uplifting testimonials guarantee absolution once a week however still can't hold a candle to charred salvation with a straight face nor complete a full sentence without a trip to the hole. Wholesale altars slash prices again yet still can't come up with a new sales pitch from prophets with bad toupees and yellow dentures. None of which should be considered germane though Gregorian chants fly through the dilapidated patchwork remorseless shuffling checkbook. Not a new dance is waltzing out the door. Capricious intentions are overreaching stretches to kindness which never go unpunished like lustful proving grounds which percolate until immediate transfer and promotion of rank and grade. Starting to come together are disparate interactions between faith and achievement which is not congruent in my playbook but everybody has their faults. Quaking in no longer wishing to eat a round is a threat of superfluous jail-time with exhausted appeals. Seeking a weathervane pointing the way to fulfillment of asinine wanderings of life examined, which contrary to Socratic foundations can be wildly overindulgent departure. Fantasizing in black and white is coming to disagreement in a gray area, further upsetting the balance that seems to be faltering in purpose. The chickens hatch and are never counted due to bad advice. A cat under-tire was a bit too laissez faire about its education. Drinking from a golden chalice is disappointment awaiting an open slot. Hands of that clock have stopped and are stabbing through future musings that have already been preempted by previously scheduled programming. Reality tv all too vivid for wild imagination beyond chasing storms in the name of meaning where nobody can define two letters, so additional information is anyone's guess. Keeping expected outcome in hands of fates and a bit of planning needs to delete the latter if the epic is to be completed within allotted time frame. If all the extras can re-coop before the final sequence renders all of the preceding just another way of homing in on a worthy task or at least logical polarity. Myopic retrospection on a collision course with nothing gained is something lost. Leaking sensitive data while withering in a carnage shot of decimated anticipations unable to conclude in anything but a non-sequitur which lost its place in line.

Irrelevant Equipoise

Inflexible forces are butting heads on the scrimmage line. Cracked helmets devour shattered dreams. Victim of self imposed drunken balancing act which teeters tenuously on devious uncalibrated fulcrums though thought tricks were for kids. Rabbits taste like chicken which could have some relevance though I've yet to discover it. Rewriting current events in an agoraphobic mask which could be found splattered on any highway. Thinking back but the chaos of dead riddles is suffering a crisis of entropic proportions. Longing for a naked lunch. Keeping tears at bay with an angry scowl and dance with a well of words dripping from an unleaded pencil. Fighting from a fortunate aerie of great tactical advantage however it's fucking up the broad strategy. Single tire on a bicycle meant for two, whatever that really means. Flying solo for all the right reasons though swing overall party lines and stomp on naive faith in mankind through desalinated eddies of cavernous peril speaking carnivorous tongue deep in promised land which never keeps its salty oaths. Breaking mundane for the deaf mute blind who haven't the senses to defend themselves while all I'm striving for is a heartbeat to sail gospel into my wanting stethoscope that would gladly return the favor. Blissful intervals between the love affair processing me to tallow, burning to the wick. Maybe a soft rub behind the ears. No doubt self-centered and callous, but blisters have a place under heaven too or perhaps above ground, which might just be half the story. Theological journalism isn't a strong suit but I try to keep up the bluff. Melting into the only seat that loves me however mercy is a missing noun. And the voices which all whisper death in raspy vocals while I dutifully scribble what I'm told. Wondering what else I can do or is this is good as it gets?

Stockholm

Rummaging through Pandora's box in a truly hair raising event and repetition of the reference takes the sting out of the evils. Can't get off on a technicality as I've penetrated the subject via ritual self-urtication for as long as my divinity has respired the fetid air of humanity. Displaying inexcusable deference to my captor though we so resemble each other, observations get a second look however it appears we coincidentally both suffer the same nystagmic disorder, rattling the lines further. Irrefutable truths are lying through their teeth while the scammers deal honest. Not given to forgive and forget because nobody does and does. Recapping an uncomfortable seating arrangement with a black rose and scratched record which doesn't even offer suggestions when spun backwards. Wondering when dissonant behavior is going to reconcile with individual determination in a happy medium which is a bit too small for me and compromise is nothing but a weaker starting point for the next round of negotiations anyway. Blasting through the ego like a tipping empire is finding seismic schisms ready to splinter into different psychic states with metaphysical ramifications. Albeit something with which I'm unfamiliar yet intuitively connected which is all just a space inhabitant for a missing conjunction at the confluence of heartbreak and freedom. Schoolhouse Rock is far gone and can't find its way home. I'm just a bill is now law of the land, jaded and bitter. All the evils gather in a semi circle around a burning star and the pedestal he's stapled to as a cross would be over the top by even Hollywood standards which of course is an assault on word pairs but seems to be holding firm under pressure from union chaplains. Remembering a picture framing lost faces and times that will never again grace grace. Subtracted from the arithmetic by an evil sibling who can't stop chewing the rag which is apparently why her gums always bleed. Married to two was one, proving more isn't always better. Reworked call to the steeple is two thousand years of separation and forget half of the aforementioned equation is gaining steam in one sided organs piping alien admonitions. Not enough fingers to count the burns. Locking away lockets in a secret spot where I can't find them. Dropping honor rolls to none as implication of expectation are the seeds of hope which is something I can't in good faith support. Finishing off a couple slices which have always made me sick and precisely the point. Devouring inedible flower which responds with quickly metabolized sweet nectar for as long as I can keep her peaks and troughs flowing tonal rhythm. Nothing else to wake up to but an increasingly bitter lady and her silicon clit. Trying to stuff the box with ventriloquist dummies as it's impossible to get all the horrors back in at once and even concealment needs prioritization. I'm not ready for visitors.

Singapore

Debating various and sundry methods by which to attack what's on the plate. Looking for odd angles to vortex and getting nowhere but spun. Cantilevered awnings demand support but the arguments are wobbly from the get go which has up and gone to more fulfilling space as wallow with my old lady is in full backswing with a tilted wrist on the follow-through. Adjusting grip midstream could be a hole in one or squeezing too tight for vindication. Logical misinterpretations have gone underground to regroup from abusive vernacular which hits a little- a little too close to home for the underwriters. Cancelled policies are interfering with principle motive which tends to flex flaccid contracts with smudged ink. Leaking sensitive material onto supple skin which is itself a revelation though doesn't require genuflected statues or bearded justice of peace which connects broken definition stampeding through a slaughterhouse. Skipping to the end can be the most logical trail when nothing's working though sunshine plays holographic tricks on functionality. Singeing prints into the vellum is one way out though tangentially fatal marks have left me targeted. Clothed daily by a sworn enemy though I'm used to being cursed by those closest. Insufficient funds in musical banks is tuckered out wind section however reeds have promised a new lead by example or at least a smack in the ass which judging by past performance is less than heartwarming and likely portends a trip to blinking lights and machines singing life so they don't start resuscitative action. No heroics is printed on my bio. Debating quality versus quantity in separate but equal is a coin rolling in eternal ambivalence. Writing myself back into the epoch though imparities are disabling any but minor combinations sounding off terminal winter. Close observation is seeing things excessively well which doesn't bode positively for abhorrent vacuum effect which is only a matter of time in the poppy fields. Examining table is gyrating on the verge of choking down too much information. Word processing has ceased accepting payment and is no longer providing collection services. Scratched pads and pointed nails would lead to belief of king of the jungle but I'd just bungle that too and have more pressing with which to cope anyway.

Exsanguinating

Ripcord or ripped cord semantic argument tumbles to cactus
finality though names have not been released. Eulogized dream
died in scrap white picket fences. Disconnect is free with a price.
Chuckling at serious brain matter offering laughable redemptive
value. Swinging from a mangrove spread of liana which tangled
beyond unchecked passenger manifest. Slicing through glass
ceiling or bled out in the process. Captive imagination is running
for a star or at least a trophy before fade to blacklist. Insolent
erstwhile philistine typing in artistic haste to avoid burgeoning
failure which is extreme in judgment though forward looking
projections are sensitive to temporary shocks no matter flowery
precedent. Inconsistent behavior is intolerable demeanor or
nature of man however it's likely the latter is an umbrella under
which the former hides from thunderstorms. Vacillating font is
reformatting the text to match esthetic offerings. Catapult dogma
misses its aim to the delight of hostage youth who now have at
least a fighting chance at affirmative formation while the
decades pass until commencement addresses serious
miscalculation of cost/benefit logisticians. Plane keeps falling
and still unsure which wing and prayer stand a better chance or
if semantics have any place in rhetorical questioning anyway.
Fearsome genetic primacy isn't playing second fiddle though
never promised anything but marquee billing the producers
refuse to remit. Chequered flag is a chessboard according to
royal doctrine but it's this type of minor hiccup that could throw
the whole irretrievably out of whack or bring work home with it.
Bursting out of encapsulated mediocrity with hopes of explosive
release though hitting eject is a knock to the head or a fast
forward to today even though yesterday hasn't been sanded yet
liberal application of uneven stain is manifest. Chasing a ghost to
even the score is walking through impenetrable walls though I
didn't make it this far without a few rocks to absorb impact.
Lasting creation is calling my name though thrown voices are a
verbal labyrinth and whence they call I have no idea.
Unwelcome formalities garner a blank stare rarely receive an
official rsvp though expletive laced diatribes hearken back to

diamond days that almost killed me and typically receive a warm welcome with a sharp retort which was really the endgame before checkmate. Taste of unbalanced unbound resolving its own vertigo. Scripture not subject to religious cooption nor mistranslation. Pipedream wishes and aborted expectation though every story deserves a punchline.

She-Devil In Red Dress

Universal corner- either meeting spot or collision in making- sometimes combination though redundant- transcendence- galactic in nature. Suggests universal congruity- implicative good beginnings ending badly. Unprecedented maneuver terminates in er- red hair burrowing through the juicy tinker into a pew- isn't party to my calendar. Absent father figure leaves firm brand. Empty frame. Innocent cover belies available data. No self respect aside profuse protestation of faith. Empty frame. Father figure wanted. Found. Too late for savior/satyr. Converse- too early for lurid blue eyes which shine jade to cast aspersion on new interest nor cleansing- only point out that determination brings laughing gods. Escaped conversation though second thought saw Ramones and red and soft- appreciating composition yet reformed whores need bit of primer before painting can begin. Spiritual orgasm requiring bit of sleep before trip to nirvana departs- opening flood gates in new form though anything is possible in his world- so I'm told. Vast lecherous thoughts. Seeking counsel with madhouse awaiting- unable to turn from princess train wreck- ETA unspecified. Stare into broken eyes- face to devour. Recalibrate distance to avoid collateral damage when lightning fries my blackened debris. Rejected by faith as I see it- given one can't command the music of heart. Assuming all is set aside for invited guests only- crashing gates out of the question. Her empty frame. Like a song never sung inside a box too well sealed to accept incoming wisdom. Such- folly of youth- as lunacy of chatting up twenty years junior. In a tree erect. Club in hand. Await morning glory coming with strawberry wind. In firm hold she begs salvation- kneels ecstatic masochist. Rosary in hand. I can only grant but brief resolution- simple momentary escape to moist frenzy- holistic- spiritual too heavy a call sign for the dig- no matter round ego. Digress- complex progressions evade. Divine lingers apparitional- so I'm told. Watches conduct- so I'm told. Empty frame. Some message from a paper I don't subscribe? Would I've been a mistake or unlikely rescue mission which aborted last minute from above?

Lived to tell about it? Salacious intervening moments render previous rhetoric immaterial?

On The Blacktop

Artistic existential is creating new rules. Plunging deeper into economical formatting which is admittedly dense and subject to appearance of connections gone MIA. Scraping by with off the wall trickery which can't find a traditional spot within the phrasing or at least al dente purchase before peeling from partitioned cookery. Care less I can't. Happy to retrieve a dictionary from the pyre which appears to be ebbing but that might indicate optimism ergo sticking with Armageddon so as not to reach too far too fast while recovering chopsticks from a plate smelling of dog or derivations thereof- fooling no-one. Indignation bonfire rises under influential bongo reverie surrounding flaming out refusing its decades. Locked horns usher in regulatory interference. Dissociative elements prominent in bounding crowd absent sinew though copious two-buck muscle. Wrapping head around heedless unwashed with two grand worth of unused shower. Speculate purpose of undulating mob of young hope staring into trick light show certain to blind ambition with unbillable promises of endless sunsets. Recap afternoon with another shot. Espresso delivery to drooling sockets begging for release of contractual obligation. Slip into twilight of caffeine immunity disorder while the shenanigans begin. Sleeping birds snore under shelter of slatted armor while Thor hammers hyper aggressive tendency- heated projectiles hailing anvil sparks. Redirect efforts in movement towards stasis. Pattern with no outline nor surface noise pointing to holy land. Steadfast adherence to rule of law is lost art which should remain on milk cartons for personal edificatory reasons among others. Licking bottom of barrel for a sip of sacrificial wine though unsure of sacrifice. Pushing in with dregs disinterested in case studies for canon bursts of criminal like matrimony. Spiked gin is an ace up the sleeve. Skip tears- nobody tastes the salt. Disinherited construction is deconstructed for upgrades. Rumor mill is sawing about game of telephone but nobody's got a quarter- another chair pulls from under dead music. Plying trade with devil is even money. No sympathy- no regret. Drooling excess in a clean-room is collecting dust in componentry. Prescribed protective gear misunderstood dosage small print. No binding treaty to stay safe- only tacit pact with mirror image projecting nothing what it looks like. Deadly dance with snake in grass seeks Kentucky Blue but only finds Memphis Slim. Pickings ripe for consumption if your stomach is strong enough for bloodshed. Unique moral code shared en masse- practice sparse. Relax-straight walks through piecemeal wall- ignore grand schism. Turn blind eye to clamming up. Stand and fight or sit and write. Job well done issues pugilistic tirades without leaving seat today- back's killing me. Opiates- MIA.

One Exit-Flying Embers

Leery of the gunning for absolution with splash and ashen forehead. Pillage six of seven moons resting on its seventh laurels while succumbing to fate of masters of inflated universes buzzing about scurrying ant like. Lapping up excess which eventually is nothing but iron too heavy to pump. Day of rest mourns the occasion. Plate-male felled by iron cross misappropriated from an unfortunate archive whose adjective might be too forgiving. Skipping beats cease function altogether in erection of next cathedral pledging a good seat in the rapture though unconfirmed reservations could be back of the bus. Fire and brimstone emissions hanging like a Damoclean dilemma over alternative means. Split ends are function of direct translation previously un-scrabbled by questionable sources of rapacious motive. Buried beneath cocksure cover is allegory of epic proportions capable of parting rivers outside amusement parks. Indiscernible magnanimity demanding alms in place of sacrifice without expectation receives failing grades from bomb shelter duck cover and roll exercise in sticky situation with cobwebs woven incredulous, is no character I would represent. Caught in random act is a missed note from a tenor. Miscalculation of the number is a beast of an issue. Spread far and wide- parish-able maps off the radar screen cloaked for security purposes. Portfolio management discrepancy revealed in unzipped confessionals with no penance offered and authority to grant hail Mary's indefinitely suspended without pay regardless. Stairway isn't a one way street should it have been approved by inspectors not on the lam or take or altar boy. Lasting implications scar evermore with indelible etchings on sacrificial souls who drank from the corroded chalice. Road to perdition is backed up to previous toll booth. Unempathetic towers show minor wear though nothing but chips off the old marble easily replaced with a trip to fine Venetian quarry where innocent bystanders dip at least tepid faith in pools rife with staph-infection. Not getting the point until too late is thin line separating glorious myth from spiteful mystic. Renounced affidavit lost its search warrant somewhere between cocktail girls on the turn home. Faithful recoil in horror-show placed face-first under icons worth more than inhabitants while fast and furious are attorneys fighting inquiring minds- eventually no avail then split to plaintiff bar with a two martini lunch followed by dessert of three more. Intractable polystyrene injections with a half short life or short half life. Frothing guilt in tridents fired from bloodshot eyes at fellow man for dopamine fix which repairs nothing. No rest for weary entrance to Monday. Pious are only letters arranged in becoming fashion diluted to have and not- as is spiritual as is charlatan as is snake-oil as is kool-aid. I run mine in a lonely journal which some call the devil's music- some say fatalistic. How exactly did they expect it to end?

Too Optimistic Still

"the urge to save humanity is almost
always a false front for the urge to rule."

~h.l. mencken

Cocksure lost mass careening off notional absurdity is stupid is
as it does which is in the script yet I fail to find the meaning any
more than celebration of lionized idiot who would likely be in
Washington with a little extra mama time pressing towards
manifest destiny of morons everywhere while preparation
knocks itself off frame before opportunity crashes the party so
that knuckleheads eat off the plates of the divinely damned
though Noah had a job too. Media-stoned glue to wicked boxes
in order to form an opinion of their own after sweat iniquity
cracking pavement in hundred degree living above the land- tar
or ivory. Pain is universal classless pox lacking an iota of
concern for station or heirloom silverware. Succumbing to the
light is a camera into my soul which is more than I wish to share
at this point on the vibrating axis excessively wont to follow
fraternal disorder tripping over tongues filthy from chase to
illusory panacea disjointed from the start by repugnant
progenitors with supremely demur mirrors permeating
Murphy's law until it proves out and logical conclusion is most
irrational outcome. Incoherent is faith in human condition.
Timeworn exemplary sampling of quotients is missing another
digit which is one step closer to losing five points of accounting
cutting the calculator at fifteen plus one which is itself
unaccounted for rendering it unavailable for ledger. Slap-tickle
parties aren't giggling. No laughing matter is individual under
influence of rabid pack voodoo dolls pricking next wink with
disingenuous calls for give a piece of filthy ass a chance while
compulsive thinkers are confined to cookery never seeming to
violate capacity restrictions though next in line cuts in to lay it
down before neurons lose connectivity and subject matter is
severed at limbic-Darwinian connection. Something like an
amputation though marred with gang tags claiming love of man

clique with wheat grass tramp stamps eating flesh of intolerable dissention that might actually elucidate a dark path but then it seems most have figured their way into and out of that hole. Box stuffed with self-determination bleeding out externalized acrimony in lieu of retrorse photography- excise taxes on final autonomy with malignant foundation on quicksand lines. Rational on every level despite lack of scientific method. Another tick on the second hand until sacred cows outnumber run of the mill which is isn't a premium blend however any port in a storm. And all one needs is to examine birthparents to catch the weather forecast before the polls close.

Black-Hole Hum

Anticoagulant penetration of stupefying ignorance lacking plan for strategic implementation is rat poison incapable of discerning vermin for the cheese crowd it is. Vivisection of side cut cat scan displays slices of stale pies. In the hole. Down in the hole. Back up the hole. Encompassing all the holes before summation abyss envelopes the universe with everybody's got one or more-meaningless to me as collective affirmation is mediocrity in popular drag however the fad will die off creating mulch for the next round if anybody can keep off the canvas without drowning in tomato soup blinding ultimate blow off the circuit. Travelling comedy troupe is finding nothing funny about blockades kidnapping vital expressive connectors separating intellectualized from visceral reaction that might have considered a bit of pre-emptive strikes itself so as not to be labeled agitator but bandwagons are enticing- especially atop rutty albeit untethered roads to redemption which could be a Spahn Ranch gig with pork on the menu and L-25 control panel monitoring drones for discounted loyalty program that's priced too steep for any but wayward undeveloped skeletons in need of marrow indiscoverable on the space time continuum for a happy ending which all points to a prophet in windowpane sugar pills. Genius is psychosis. How many lurk? Burnout is rubber on the road or quick trip down under though I don't speak Aussie. Too many balls in the air is either an overloaded schedule or promiscuous queer. Skipping conjecture which tends to corral phobia while insulting as much doctrine in need of dispelling as possible. Besides- homos don't scare me though their petrified politics splinter what's left of lucid or right of madness whichever comes first however politics bore me to ulcer. Limited time is sucking itself into 'the clock's ticking sweetheart' gargled through excessive makeup shouting too much protest to belie the lacerations on her pasted face- right to left off the map when empire building implodes. Televised card wars are tipping the scales of obvious tells into coffers of entranced between commercial interruption or disruptive train wreck killing dozens though even splayed fingers avoid looking past the remote which finds purchase on home shopping network thereby releasing liability for disasters from the social contract which I never signed- picking up a set of grails machine engraved with a Plutonian signature for a song to boot. Rules of chance dealing nanny cradles just enough info to present clear and present danger to the entire system. Near invariable underestimation of dim cerebral activity burning candles of streaming trivia at both ends of top stories while adding nothing but a contradictory subtractive element implicating sub-zero integral temperature if the math is paying any attention at all and differential solutions are medically impossible due to potential for frostbit when appendages are spread during remediation procedure. Solid chain mail is weighing down body and soul in inconsequential receipts. Throngs of ineptitude bounce off the words in favor of silver platter handouts which are scrapped at tin value that approximates the sum-worth of collective bargaining agreements exclusive of protected speech which is that tandem to inherent source code function of collective zeitgeist that never seems to be in good spirits. Suddenly old Chuck is looking well kempt in appropriate surroundings- as stated, likely buys me a first class seat to a fiery river crossing- better to throw honesty in dying wind than fable into eternity which probably won't like me any better than the apparitions sleeping on my shoulder- not that I don't already have a premier boarding pass anyway. Temporarily mistaken for Atlas when gazing into summarized analysis intended for someone's benefit yet the belief is cratered by another tragedy which drops a boulder onto the wrong soundstage during filming- killing gods and mortals alike which could be immaterial distinction if one is parasitical tag-along in heart of the other.

Over The Flame

Unforgivable trespass a decade in formation is finding mitigation beginning pullout of retrorse troops from the heart of darkness. Cancelled checks deep in statute of limitations have no recourse afforded too many luxuries though a second hand in the ointment is equally responsible for the contamination. Spiral to unforgiving retribution in form of carved visibility with no inclination for fame breaks fall on winged ascent. Scraping by with more than a couple scratches as passing meteors mark their hunting grounds with an unmistakable odor of seared flesh. Graphic delusions of the night resemble reproductions so true to form that photo copies are available in trailers for a sequel likely to be succeeded by another though success is far from certain. Rapping silent knuckles with an invisible ruler taking on the simulacra of penance however resembles nothing begging forgiveness as lashes whip internal spirit where my deities lie therefore it's gods taking the abuse with each inverted ticket stamp. Crying over spilled milkshake is child's play or not enough thereof which has a tendency to interfere with conscripting social contract. Head spun around metaphysical loom is asking whether the construction of the windmill obligates the blades. Forgotten interjection is on the tip of missing tongue long talking in confused dialectic which bounces off itself at critical junctures impossible to expound upon with poor wiring firing off again so feel free to fill out the questionnaire as you see fit omitting no perceived detail crucial to your side of the story. Words no longer hold meaning after anything bakes to anything but me. Open accounts don't bear witness to internal struggle nor author release of demand obligations of notarized dotted lines from a mound above a depleted quarry. Two adding up to no beginning nor end went out to tango a modular half scale dance floor suspended over a shark pool and were never again seen in standard format. Spatial awareness can be either alert to surroundings or cramped conditions with fashionable outcroppings leaving too little to imagination among other things. Could just be internal investigation that never begins which is a red mark on a blotter or a ship at risk of sinking under the weight of all the worlds with nary a clue as to which to point my joystick at first. Deep in process of fashioning a crown of thorns for dramatic effect is shut down by inspectors on the take for whatever they can cop. Impeccable timing for once not covered in glaze upon arrival as contradictory reports call into question verdict and sentence. Forming a revised opinion is new found disregard and a page from Camus. Ain't my fucking problem anymore. In your incompleteness is the downside of a great blow-job. Wipe your facial before you throw more salt. Adrift in renewable philosophical pursuits. Maybe befriend a scaly winged beast or two in the process. It'll all come out in the wash like a backroom deal leaving a stack of intestines by the screen door. Then again you never did look back but for bank statements.

Tell Me Who Owns Who

American nightmare just purchased absolution in form of larger quarters to stock with superfluous bullshit once hoping to find its way into use before obsolescence. Gathering history in musty corners is no way to utilize highest and best use. Overbearing depressive tendency is stuck to a sofa sitting on treasure trove of galvanized implosive devices yet can't blast through stone. Skinning knees on whatever it is I'm sinking my teeth into though she's rarely grateful however turn-about is fair-play so not to discount strict compliance with social etiquette. Wrapping legs around subject is wrestling in Portuguese or brain-drain quagmire with no visible means of excision. Third option is out of order for overdue regularly scheduled maintenance sleeping through eviction notice. Disinterested observation is perking up at assignment of blame. Irrational sidestep can't pass a sobriety test. Rearranged atmosphere is history's bookmark. Oversized egos on undersized lots in hand over fist chase to end of the bat and the last Jones has been accounted for. Subliminal suggestions are overt demands of an outlet center near you or spin the wheel with no reservations but plenty of firewater. Depraved difference is nabbed by the feds after co-conspirators agreed to rat trap the only honest one in the bunch. Target acquisition doesn't cost anything rather a credit on the books. Supplying lyrical background ambience is so far off key nobody can get in the door except with boundless capacity for forgiveness. Exclusionary blue properties on a monopoly board stream unconsciousness which is better left to professionals or finger paint. Drying up like a witching hour in the desert is not an option. Unavoidable cracks in the arid mud manifest in missing hikers which could just be fugitives on the lam or needy desolation evening the score. Uninvited guests smell like penultimate section of a yarning which got away. Superglue wasn't a birth-name but changed in fear of association. Any club that would have me is out of their collective mind which I suppose is why none do. Tell it to your priest- your transgressions which march in woeful silence from forgotten trifles to frontal lobe- pierced and defiled. Shred it if you will and it seems certain your trip to better places will drag the whole magilla under. Shards of contrivances are hot coals under manifestly optimistic footing which won't share air-time with anything not bounding in nonsensical toothy glee despite seething review. Can't abide whatever it is that I refuse to obey. Lacking the slightest modicum of decency or good intentions when speaking truth so mastering solitude to avoid telling lies which would only serve to ingratiate nobody within my solipsistic boundaries while sucking from existential commands leading to heaving dry hyperbole into a bowl that doesn't care but can carry a scent longer than I can handle the odor without repercussion. Denying access to sensitive information for fear of nothing except boredom of inaccurate translation. Speak no evil hear no evil or perhaps it should be- ask nothing you don't want to know and you won't know it which should simplify matters immensely. Filling coffers with useless is traditional rite of passage prematurely leading to a triumvirate of ritualized scoops which certainly cleans up the calendar though forsaken attics particalize in light of survivors who will faithfully carry on the tradition of possession is nine tenths of whatever possesses you.

Land Of Free Despots

Final frontier at odds with current requirements charging electrified air into a weathered lighting rod. Direct despot is deceitful solution which won't hold up to check your answers- admittedly treads losing traction- though the natives gather in wigwams planning insurrection or at least a flash mob at the Capitol. Dislocated slices of diminishing global threat is a boon to natural order which sees light across a tunnel of fourteen billion feet. Immunosuppressant elements won't allow for many additional sequels after the first two bombs. Planning sessions of bacterial contingents are focused on hit 'em where it counts. Could start with med-schools to attack the problem at its source- stem the flow of injectable warfare- however gooey consistency holds a masochistic streak or solid improvisation- seems enemy is often as confused as issue-voting. Scoundrel phantoms are eerie reminders. Superior intellect is death of a nation. Degreed pedigree is sure sign of malfeasance or close enough for government work. Efforts to contain the din are met with scowl and tornado. Talking heads bobbling their way around dicey situations are increasingly at risk of getting cut up and smoked like squares. Impinged blood-flow is tearing at her divide and not doing much for spirits writhing among themselves in blind ambition for something untouchable despite best efforts and six rabbits' feet. Even good luck gets a day off. Sullying reconstructive surgery has taken it off the agenda yet few possibilities remain for the mundane- the status quo which seems to take station a bit too literally for my taste though job will lecture next week and likely present a more measured outlook on parallel universes crashing headlong into their doppelgangers creating a hybrid illegal in all states but Kentucky. Well, perhaps West Virginia though we're still looking for a translator to dissect the statute. Too close for comfort are hormonal cousins on a Lazy-Boy. Cat scratch fever is spreading like hairballs. The rivers are muddy debates- tributaries await victor before alliances are affected. Lasting accords keep until the medics are called. Broken boards are in casts though shall rise soon as the anesthetic wears off.

Inevitable invariably laughed off while she tilts her folds ever so slightly so as not to alert environmental do-gooders who've accomplished little but vast motorcades and private jet fumes which is ok by me for overbought and oversold indications are historical proof or at a minimum strong anecdotal evidence. Monarchy in danger of collapse should fold its cards and start over. First order- disarm Bloomberg's guards. Better yet- disarm Bloomberg.

Tear It Down

Rocket's red glare drones back to unmanned video game imported from Japan to occupy time at Crystal Mountain or whatever facility they moved into last. Signal flares are targeted for annihilation. An SOS is read as pessimistic. They're moving in- the acronyms- at the will of blinded by the satanic light which is typically beyond what might be considered my expertise though finding a comparable adjective is hoping for a genie to exit a lamp that hasn't even been rubbed. Intercepted communication could be a novena or voter intervention. Revenue agents are generating solid returns and can't go public or risk profit-sharing. Enraptured in cable images of their own ineptitude is high flying low risk pastime. Undiscoverable until too late to prosecute is executive order resulting in potential execution of last will and testament which is a multiple choice question with no correct answer. An apple fell from a tree and from this- the seeds of counterintelligence proving its name and complete lack thereof knocking perforated holes in Chad or some other African state. Wondering where the booths are but they've been replaced by holes in the ground. Power to the people is a generating plant but not much more. Scapegoating another platform is gridlock which is admittedly preferable than free reign though asymptotic difference of opposing polls requires a microscopic view to verify the shrunken chasm. All of which is implicit of a bloody Mary with modern attachments to the doctrine long lost in the Sahara however Indiana is busy searching scripture for clues and the ark is still missing notwithstanding cut and paste brushed under the rug that lies through it's shag. Withstanding any and all attempts at silencing death for certainty is secured so why bother walking that line unless it's early ejection desired? Two technicals and a manual shift in tide is repeating what bears no repetition which does so at will anyway which again makes one wonder why bother. Slowing functionality is currently smacking extreme exhaustion which isn't to imply sparing any harsh vernacular however articulation is subject to sub-par rounds that isn't in this case a positive walk towards the house. Not sure when there was one though I could get out of my chair and stretch if someone decides to march up DC for anything other than a million anything for or against something. Preferable- lone soldier on lectern with bullhorn announcing my indifference towards gone missing. Sometimes necessary acts require a big sack of virile. Lucky for everyone involved I've flat feet releasing me from liability or i swear... Regularly. I'd hate to drone on regardless.

Descent

Scurrying hordes of discontent running through gauntlet of just another day. Scampering about in pained daze across a painted landscape on abysmal canvas. Seems the buses burn cleaner yet lack the character of old Hollywood which I'm not sure was much better than its progeny but for fuck's sake it can't be any worse than the stagnant cesspool which walks red carpet of its victims who call out in warning though nobody listens. Hemlines are failing their charge which is apparently their goal. Daddy's little girl gone modern whore chic. Pigtailed brat is future manipulative genius which is intuitive part of nature but I can't seem to work up the energy to examine the whole in any fashion that would render the analysis just and may just damage pride in the process. Fate worse than life is tyrannical subservience. Forty six percent paying some percent in interest adds up to nearly fifty percent of budgeted expenditures which is to say that nobody has a fucking clue as to the extent of fucking ourselves over we have become accustomed to while blackened lungs prepare for what can never come due to time constraints. Abstraction is apparently lost in the lines here which means I'm being less opaque than normal serving as no comfort whatsoever. Digressing into more familiar confines is somewhere in the rafters laughing ghoulish at the farce below being played out like an off-Broadway understudy circus and yes they are fucking clowns. I hate clowns. They rule the fucking clowns. I hate clowns. Locked in transition is yellow to white. Hatred spews from the hearts south of the DMZ which should become an MZ without foreign interference but then nobody listens to me about a fucking thing and who could blame them? Incessant invective rambling is either early onset mania or slow healing life dynamic. Don't hear any horns blowing my name but a hiss or two seems to be sounding off at variable intervals which I surmise could be a furnace type thing though the heat is central so I keep on my toes. Distracted by snake-oil and palm readers is keeping from given task which is laying waste to everything- especially rumors of membership in ugly infighting sect of acrimonious tribal contingencies which couldn't be further from the truth as my application has yet to be approved. Seems there's red-tape in purple states too. I always liked grape though. Won't die gleeful likely but won't be riding a desk as the world goes round in blips of off kilter indications and torrents so incessant as to beg catching their own breath- demanding all mine- sometimes actually meaning something but I forget what exactly which is a lie but dead and buried and nothing can adequately charge the synapses so why cry over scrambled cortex? Inscription might do but to that I subscribe- upon second look am not quite sure what that pertains to but it is written- ergo it's too late for change- redactions make me retch. Won't be caught dead walking-dead in a steady of flow of Brooks Brothers demanding descending escalators for a change of direction but careful what you wish for. Won't allow current lucidity to impact my diatribes as waxing sense goes over even worse. Will laugh tears of tear as the whole plays out but the dirge has been written and none too soon. Procrastinating the dentist prolongs agony. Will lobby stalwart for withdrawal from 38th parallel or at least effect hospitality instruction for K-Town work permits. Can only engage so many battles as manifest in this twisting manifesto- the flight attendants are drafting half the plane for vouchers to which nobody will affirm and a rocket launcher to be named later.

Defrocked

Land of opportunity lost its chance but who can be surprised? Hard rain befalls empires. One world nonsense is divided inflection point. Regrouping is searching for records of the group though can't see past partisan cocktail. Drunk and orderly is only half right. Central syncopation with whole is largest heist played on man since original sin deemed us murderers of someone we never met. Not on paper anyway though the parchment is plethora of indication. Large samplings are ignorant masses. Sapling ideology- young hope or conveniently lost senses. Assassinating all values is costly diversion though keeps fluids pumping until the great escape chutes into Laos or perhaps Geneva. Reincorporated tactics are sequels to failed premieres. Large scale isn't holding up its end of the bargain though counting calories overloads the calculator anyway. Stuck somewhere between 'it doesn't look good' and 'stop drop and roll' is an eight ball set to automatic sagacious. Repeating same rag may be a drag but overwhelming absurdity is a tough chew. Consequential trips up the fret-board are certain as twelve bar blues. Lighter shade of pallid is an apparition. Ghost of what once was but looking forward is same as looking back until a millennial leap in genetic pre-releases. Pardoning my sin for a moment however it seems supplication is human interdiction where simple grace would do and not aggravate bulging discs upon standing. Spinning old tracks to remind me of my expanding timeline which is self negating around the central point. Dissecting each and every connection for the standings though box scores are harder to come by. I'm hearing call of wild mountains rustling discomfort at next administration as fuck me once can still get pregnant. Rapping on incessant about insurrection may seem a bit too close to Montana for some though big skies open through small clouds. Rewriting insufficient funding has me on the black list which is darker than radar evasive. Scalping my way into a new state which is running black water holding tanks on fire. Acidic discharge can't keep it down any longer. Attempt at actively evasive of confrontation though it's all a journey- isn't it?

Forgiveness is tiring of the penance. Locking doors on old scheme which is dead on arrival of first compromise. None of it will matter at the end of matter as we know it. Big bang is both the genesis of all energy ever created and spandex-splitting hustle. Inanity of ontological dissertation is an acquired taste with a steep tag though a clutch of points to hang next to autodidact diplomas from institutions of higher learning which sink into dubious hypotheticals. Splitting is a marriage made in heaven. Perhaps the twisters are telling us something. Not in Kansas anymore? Maybe it just landed you in a better place which would have to be far from here there or anywhere on the decay which is earth hyped up on human and looking to kick the habit. Perhaps a frock too.

Righting The Wronged Ship

Subjugation of one persona under cover of subordinated indebtedness is effort to hide underwritten anomaly which is actually as common as snot-faced toddlers vying for more air-time. Electrified wasp nest is setting stage for sanctions. Lasting pacts becoming tacit ambiguities. They're listening from above. Reading engorged ether traffic plus a cool jam where thought appropriate. Carving new identities may be advisable though could be recurring course of requisites. Common reflection of national movement is function of external opposition or dearth thereof. Drool on the flagged casket of apple pie lost to the ages whose world-view will be a revised edition which is best we can hope for. Sacrificing liberty for a temporary sense of security begins axiomatic contention from this side of Franklin Ave. Discussing alternative means of reestablished relations are differing in preferred source of capital. Founding father is a tombstone. Ageless plot is showing neglect. Rounding too many corners to keep the train rolling on the same track but hoping to end at the same station or risk delayed legislation which is the only acceptable conclusion anyway so can't understand why I'm concerned about punctuality rather than stark-raving-mad expressionistic conjecture. Slipping into commentator mask is subject to rapid interdiction so maybe I should only keep the twenty or so disguises I know of or won't shut up which tends to prove they're there regardless of what they have to say for their opinion is theirs and worthy of a fair hearing though no Irish women are available. Inane couplets too big for the crib notes barking lengthy diatribes without fear of reprisal nor dogmatic. Straight line denied its linear nature is a missing link which is the snake that bit as you leafed the wavering answer key. Denying trends is sure way to destitution. Lesson plans focused on current events failing to illuminate the sordid past which is but a hint of the future if the atomic clock keeps solid time in Greenwich or anywhere else once the blade drops our collective heads onto red velvet which is all recorded and stored for future reference in a stealthy warehouse manned by spitting cobras of chameleon ancestry.

Rattling in nearby bushes confirms unionized enemy of the state. Not making time predictions but the cicadas are singing excessively morbid though in perfect time. Not if but when is counting the minutes. Halting of monolithic ships is measured in miles. How many years in a mile? Time to change costumes is a variant of perceived threat level. Hope they don't take my abstinence for incoherence. I leave that to them.

Astigmatic

Fallacy of history books is failing current and future prognostication elective. Defraying costs of excess spending by playing hocus pocus with the books which are fined for having no solid cover story to mask missing elements. Discarded foible shouts from doleful streets. Nobody will accept culpability resulting in a snapped compass. Misplaced inflection points to steadfast philosophical view which happens to have the cat by the tail despite cries of foul from the bleachers. Scabbing through the lines is stuck in the tape. Recapitulating is giving in again. Reaping high and mighty from an apple tree is ego's first appearance. Dance-hall days are spinning their dates in back seats whose time honored tradition has no respect anymore. In ghouls' clothing chapter after chapter could be straight trip to bottom of happy go lucky fantasy section though elevation to prophet earning respect isn't impossible any more than flying pigs. Divulging innards in scattered mounds is only way to slip past the censors. One-way alleys invite two-way traffic as long as nothing is leaked in the political press. Disinterested in altercations is calling for a truce though obstinate aggressive refuses to budge. Not party to any party. To any community. Any society. Recalcitrant progression is contrived euphemistic wing on a prayer lacking so much as a snowball's chance in hell but then I'm biased against conveniently misinformed or plain hypocritical. Unfortunate self-induced myopic consortium deems dissention as mutiny on the bounty of a lectern which itself refuses to listen to the sickness that is the mob in heat any longer- perhaps proving their point about keeping out riff-raff or unapproved rhetoric. Burying any expectation for greatness is watering impressionistic with poor visionary attitude and worse eyesight. Pond lilies are still life comparisons. Today is yesterday redux- tomorrow is today tweaking. Inseparable conceptualizations are confusing the crowds which comes as no surprise though even small bits of hope can leave big holes. Gaping wounds failing faith seeking god with gauze or perhaps it's nothing more than a scraped elbow on the way there. Blatant inconsistencies are thickening up my thoughts into mortar immovable but by force of taken off the bill which is fine with me. Close thy doors now for there may be no later. Speaking in other tongues gets my vocal chords evicted from their airy castle. Sand gets old after a couple corndogs anyway. Remember?

Dissolve

Surreptitious rendezvous at a theater near you proving respect is a water soluble concept. Previously inconceivable now a just another day until. Refractory illusion bends expired calendars into increasingly vociferous discretion which isn't using good judgment. Another song hits like a side of beef and bleeds all over any mere suggestion of at least attempting deceitful with propriety- instigates a kick to the bucket which feels like my full male dialogue has been rammed up my throat. Laughable excuses are choking on their spit while I stew over grand nothingness. A jaybird is making somnambulant passes around not much of a postcard- waking up with a stranglehold on whoever's filling in. Moths are going hungry in starving closets and the watch just struck a deal to lie to me though I'm on to myself. Skipping rocks across moonlit water isn't much of a walk in the park but it does yelp questions. Four out of five respondents offer a favorable review to a deep unmarked grave though three don't even know me. Paranoid trip is looking over its shoulder for the bullet that will get him. Cruising through another day of academia which is attempting to hold hostage last vestiges of loathing but doesn't much have the heart for it anymore. Days are standing so still that they persist to surprise me upon arrival. So still that they've yet to inform me of the advanced state of the year which is moving along quite rapidly despite the fact that it's waylaid in another eternity which doesn't much care for this one so writes a new ending yet to be approved by the studio. Racing to the next chapter is way off the bookmark but those menus are confusing. World of no craft is plying an evil trade which is blessedly rewarded then you lose perspective and accompanying parties to be named between the lines. Then you die. Everywhere in between but a lugubrious pit-stop which can't grin despite medical evidence. Rummaging old wardrobes now smelling of mold. Enticing fragrance counter reeks of a catchy pop hook to a mouth of music whose taste won't leave the subconscious now and forever- which is another subject altogether but suffice it to say the world is square no matter proof of the contrary. Successively larger concentric circles within confines of the box are uncalculated margins which seem to be a sticking point for the multitude stuck there as calculating the area requires use of applied calculus few ever knew and fewer still would know how to apply as directed on the rainbow packaging. Besides- that tree was going to fall whether or not we chose to watch so its easier just to turn the other cheek and pretend the horizon doesn't jump from the edge. Shaking my head as my heart yawns- wondering still how emotional collapse was mistaken for mental inferiority other than a likely defense of slow uptake perpetrators which might be an amusing twist yet not unpredictable or approaching invalid. Especially in the company of a coupla two bit actors who really never cared about character development anyway? Try grasping mercury. May as well have expectations only pure childhood and retardation are privy to for chrissakes. Hell- might as well be an optimist exploring thin ice on a pogo-stick.

All Too Visible Hands

Odd word pairings are divorcing like hummingbirds. Slapped injunctions aren't producing desired results. Unintentional slip of the tongue is unable to recite the alphabet. They tell us it will all be ok under their stewardship. Nothing more to say on the subject for truth is self-evident so skip into an alternate being with borderline expressions. Impressed into the alternator is a bug in the system. Lost in a transmutative state which is quickly changing its tune. Under pressure of systemic overload belching its excess. Tiring of infernal abuse of process. Unincorporated defiling of bread and butter produces disenfranchised. Hobo expedition is lost though no search party has been dispatched. Mountains of gold have been leveled for the common good or just to protect children from childhood. Illegitimate is a contradiction within a term. Encapsulated theory is bursting from its shell however nobody's all too excited to see the full report. Rapping over lapping tides but I refuse to lick any toads. Conspicuous consumption is hallucinating without my assistance. Search for whole in empty comes up with nothing to allow for either. Repealed ethical formations are stalactites caving under the pressure. Increasing abstract proportional weight is pre-diabetic though lack of sugar in explication is capping reality in pancreatic purgatory. Scalping tickets to my funeral at a convalescent hospital. Flapping gums are sticking to enamel veneer which won't hold up the bridge after a breached levee is taxed to a plea bargain. Skipping rope in lieu of other means which isn't to imply pending action just redundant glass to be broken in case of emergency. Repetitive motion has tennis elbow. Mild dissociative disorder is switching to a stronger blend despite best attempts. Premature maturation can't act like an adult. Noncompliant prisoners of Orwellian horror show are asking for different uniforms but they were all burned in the great purge. Atypical exploitation of time honored tradition has no respect for heritage. Lacking reasonable explanation of inconsistent translations has me seeing stars though fame never impressed me. Bubble above the caption says shake well for best use however I needed a bonded Laotian translator to interpret.

When all else fails avoid the directions. Trojan horses come in many tongues.

Youth Gone Child

Igniting a votive candle without a prayer of a chance encounter as my novenas sing far away to cosmic dust though could be Gregorian chants however one can't tell over thump of gravitas on foreheads. Neither croons for my type anyway so no reason to get up in coat of harms. Straw dog ambiguities are neither here nor there past expiry rather elucidation of lifeless traveler in solipsistic universe which won't suffer intrusion upon the only thing that exists. Decrying logical conclusion is manifest inanity. Slaughtering hopes is looking for a victim. Texture of missing gristle isn't tactile sensation. Overnight madness is grabbing for a pistol only to awake to an empty chamber. Terminated for cause is questioning because. Uncircumventable oval is hurling spinning wheels into the cheap seats. Standing in wait is playing roulette with a failed concept though conceptual failure is epidemic and likely endemic to the species. Recalibrating slide-rules to allow for drafting outside the lines. Creating artistic is beating an innocent child who splatters skull in painted daydream or eviscerated shards with ligature marks covering carved memos to self. Forgotten generation is heralded by frothing marketers. Early years peddled for narcissistic satisfaction which is explained as all that matters. Revolution beginning and ending with a star in its own eye poison ground water beneath rows of tombstones etched with self-indulgent epitaphs leaving out the salacious details which might detract from the redacted epoch. Footsteps of destruction are sown with no intention but self gratification which loses gusto as reference points grow fuzzy and what remains only shells out a shadow of former self. Perpetual scream at die-cast replications which may bear no resemblance to unquestioned portrait yet does however put a scarlet letter on the erstwhile pious while I enumerate transgression from behind a spotting scope. Not mine to judge doesn't apply to ostensible blaspheme or those who don't care to dabble in semantics. Requisite hole in pocket for the cause is leaving hunger for future panels to tackle once the legal proceedings have completed the cover-up which is slip of the tongue measured in billions and billions served up on a silver platter for pedophiliac-only confessionals though conflict of interest leaves the other side closed until further notice so a couple of hail-Marys will have to do until the next field trip. Road to salvation is beset by many who would mine the path to a meaningful mea culpa though nobody's really sorry for what they do until judgment day or a look down my barrel which could be one in the same were I offered a crown of thorns. Were I disposed to impose sanctions while sleeping dogs lie and their prophecies are called into question.

Another Trip Goes Down On America

Beset by multitude of uninvited guests frothing on pending departure. Tracking down the source of karmic dislocation is lost between consequence and deed which is apparently a four letter word. Last in uninterrupted schedule of non-committal mandated into the crime. Starting again from day one twice in a row. Undeterred progression of regressive enigmas eating at far end of time served despite hooded caveat spitting unpleasant into craven expression denying itself its weakness. Concerned with fate of universal disinterest is apathetic with a short fuse. Crazed vagabond is forced dissipation of Mexican spices in fine mist- blinding what would be innocent if there were such a fantasy as sight while the limbs keep swinging. Borderline moron exacting revenge on past life though I'm unsure of apologies I might owe the fates. Guessing it could be worse though not looking gift horses in the mouth since it's been beaten past passed much as insufferable sentient repression. Succumbing to push forward in kinder light pulls internal monologue into soundproof quarters while myopic brimstone clouds the lens. Accusations of irretrievable commentary shoots itself in the foot which should be buried deep in a closet with the rest of the bones before the house is torched for good however no such luck is axiomatic actuarial. Taking no as my answer isn't coming across in a positive fashion though running out of time isn't necessarily out of style. Speaking from first party standpoint is holding position though agitating rhetorical episodes are testing peeling geography with not an onion of a chance. Peace through power is a solid concept though never accounts for free-will which is almost invariably quite costly and could lead to execution of the former syllable. Getting out of chair is fair warning though nothing in the syllabus of Thorazine university is parting the clouds. Pulling out is no option after mangled factions balloon the dynamic. A little compromised makes strange bedfellows with ardent ideal. Arrival of dignitaries notable only for numbers departs what should be a grey goose but pin-stripes belie true intention and fitting wardrobe. Dead fish reaches for buried fighting words pocketed in invisible ink. Dead ringer for leading asshole in height is claiming bankruptcy but we already knew that. Spanish newscast is getting banged from byline to story and back though can't be too pleased with unscarred troller regardless of voter indiscretion or simple genealogical law of large numbers if glad hands aren't slapping a tickling fancy. Appalled ego deflated by request for identification responds with dismissive attempt at superior air which smells much like a bid for higher office but could just be disbelief that sound-bytes without amplification are trees that never fell in these woods. Directional miscues are debating karma's relationship with luck which may have merit yet serves no purpose. Interpersonal ends where a step forward encourages a leap from my seat which prefers indolence but will take the scene as a final cut and act accordingly. Another finale under a redundantly suspicious moon is a phantom menace which may climax in yet another sequel type reprisal or simply ghoulish organs piping death rattles into nod.

Independence Splayed

Approaching fireworks are the end of time. Astrological mystic is bullshit and I'm only buying all of it. Approaching planetary realignment is skinning my bones. Given immeasurable statutory law of large numbers and wide chasms of potential mitigation, I'm trying to obviate a poor track record which doesn't have many pleasant hooks to catch a wide audience. Paranoia uber alles but it doesn't mean they haven't fallen below with a shank in the back. Intertwined emotional content is again outside looking in on stand-up falling flat on its face in a pagoda mirror so the review may be subject to more favorable scrutiny. Stink-eye coming from a side of beef is prelude to a mix. Catapulting inertial indifference into the cocktail is excessively tired and capitulates to aging moments. Retracting some liability from underlying implication is displacing the water which is formless though my kung-fu is poorly lacking. Tango under flashing lights where the bats crack and the organ grinds secular division is a ticket to a ride which couldn't go the distance. Assignment of blame is too much homework. Cancelled options are lost derivatives which can't find their way home. Unsealed ring of fire lights a devil sky breathing sulfur revelry into questionable historical dimensions. Stray missiles part entranced onlookers before impaling me with a day I sensed but never saw. Cutting it down to 364 would screw up the whole mechanism so I'll watch it burn down once a year and still never catch the conflagratory days in purgatorial limbo. Will chase my own tail with full knowledge of pointless action though inertial incapacitation dictates must do something even if spinning wheels while the city burns my eye like the pepper spray I sucked doing a good deed just the other night. Clichés are there for a reason. Use them with care but don't be shy. White clouds are on the run. Charred construction hiding any benevolent power created before or after big bang turns to shield its eyes from the terror. Lying in formless immobility is a suit looking much like my twin only my lawyer is named Lucifer and I signed on for the consequences. The lights rain like lethargic gumdrops with a mission to complete. Pyrotechnic malfunction knocks out the streetlamps. The show's been taken off the air for good. Feels like the Fourth of July. Here and now. On this plane- even though it crashed and burned so long ago.

Tackling A Grizzly

Is archetype of self a paradigm or just a collection of smaller epochs to be summed up in the protoplasmic math rendering the amalgam of the standards the actual cover model for timid starlets which are masters of a smaller castle within imminent domain of psyche semantics? You're an enigma trapped within a multi-variable equation that was supposed to be a riddle but mercury slips the fingers like dead moons and I have no interest in tethering greased pigs nor swaggering swine. Can selective memory get spontaneously bombed so as to stagger past frozen sunsets? Slithering into my Gila lounge in what could be referred to as coming out of the sun though depleted energies are tripping breakers in onyx waves. Sprinkling no light on a universe which condescends its own luminescence upon unreceptive principles and more than occasionally excessive ambivalence. Jumbled ruminations appearing in alphabet soup though something connects them much as monkeys typing all books ever written if given space and time which is albeit extreme though concealing truth within simplistic dissertations is baring all for a measly couple bucks while abstract tendency daubing splashed diversions of the muse turned apathetic towards bush-league attempts at translation. Increasing optimism is a ruse to keep traffic up however changing fatalistic absurdism into humanistic progressive which nobody would believe for good reason anyway is a non-starter with bad alternate plotline flat-lining in a buckshot heap. Unfurled brows are showing dimples of contemplation. Scrapping any and all albums without completely destroying the records. Masticating a rotten deal in acidic reminders of a master of all that liberated the wheels their screech but couldn't grasp the fundamentals even with an elementary level test rebroadcasted to elucidate the issue in ten easy hash-marks all of which i refused to check despite exclamation points piercing me from every angle of the flat-screen. Are these the work of archetypical componentry such as an overactive superego attacking my every action with a sneer or are they just building blocks of the whole prototype itself? In other words can the essence of ruptured beginnings be in themselves the model of primary example with the latter getting all the credit? The plot stealing thematic license from headline players behind the lens under the scaffold. Top billing charging too much for collecting recyclables in futile hopes of aping delusional impossibility- more casting an animated sculpture bringing Rodin to tears than Cervantes swinging from a windmill without so much as a rope or tire. Archetypical delusion or delusion of archetype?

Solo Actor

Quasi anarcho-libertarian existential absurd Atheist Jew with fatalistic misanthropic tendencies exploring a more concise definition though peeling labels provoke a touch and go situation like retracted landing gear invoking a belly-landing which likely culminates in one survivor. Solipsistic wholeness is narcissistic non-recognition pact or snickering at massive inconclusiveness which doesn't exist. Dissonance had children and resultant obliterative obviation of widely distributed grumbling of primary numbers is redistricted into singular pursuit. Inadvertent slip of the lung is a stain on a red white and black box promising temporary reprieve from the battle cries though sobs into burnt out ashes aren't succeeding at quenching the fires of knowledge of unattained or at least a couple good questions. Entanglements with balls of twine are mistaken for no perceptible connections though the world isn't for the faint of heart so congruent underpinnings command transfiguration of rhetoric to offset simpleton print which isn't necessarily a positive as simple is low-road television wiping perspiring decision from obligatory working draft- reciting one's resolute opinion without subjective assistance, requiring little effort beyond a snap of the bottle and click of a remote so as one needn't make threats related to getting out of the chair. Abbreviated work day is lower pay-grade or a coat left next to a time-clock of amnesiac predisposition once the whistle blows. Inescapable truths are hanging from a briar's gallows by their Mensa standings. Recumbent thematic representations are taking a step backwards to check the mirror and trying to adjust the ties that bind however the director won't acquiesce now or forever. Universal indifference is hidden under cover of it doesn't exist for it has yet to be allowed in the soloists attic while the narcissist decries inattention to detail whirling in an orbit of presumptive obligation of galactic intervention on his behalf. Redistributive measures are the buck that gave at the office. Overly abundant internalizations are gaining weight while exo-skeletal operations appear in disarray which may terminate erection upon future inspection. Steadfast principles have been downgraded to equivocation to maintain backstage credentials. Unwelcome dictations are packaged like the addiction coughing up philosophical allusions well above time and grade which never feel their age and swear the blood tests were rigged. Scampering the fields of the only thing that lives is tougher than appearances tend to illustrate however I did graduate from picture-books. The rest is hazy however as you don't exist it would seem I'd only be clearing my own air. Plight of foundation with too much water in the mix would be disastrous though muddy connections of family members are distinctions with little difference- therefore bordering on the redundant-something familiar at least while I take the knots out of the yarn woven into a corner that is tilted polling. They'll still hate me but at least have reason. Then again- they don't exist, so why go on but to fill a page and hope for a succeeding note with a hint of viability while the wind section is all bagged up and ready to split? Bananas in the mezzanine are waking the dead. I'd never know it. I am me- the whole in its rubble entirety. Nice place to live in theory though the taxes are steep.

Dashing Home Which Isn't

Five thousand miles has nothing on the infinite- my distance from home. Wondering where to find exact coordinates is turning into a real mind-bend but no spoons follow suit. Reacting to situational awareness with a lethargic yawn until blocked depth perception trips the wire and swipes the card. Incumbent sociological statutes take the fun out of the game but the relief pitcher never seems to throw his weight around efficiently. Jack-off of all trades attempting mastery of one running on borrowed type. Lasting impersonations are eternal representations- often misspeaking in the wrong patois though confused mono-linguistic only volunteers objection in the key of mute flat. Convention metamorphoses to a melted puzzle whose corners have been rounded to increase difficulty points. Rotating on a new axis which isn't an allusion to powers that were but rocket's red glare illuminating malevolent droning sources that wish not to be named though the cat's out of the bag and clawing for more. Surreptitious waterboarding now out of the question though they're too many tapes to burn in the allotted time anyway. Febrile killer-bees working doubles to make haste though can't dent the bottleneck of first amendment corpses landing in their honey though how any of this relates to anything is a question of many zeroes and won't be broken down to bits other than to say for now I'm free to scribble infernal nonsense which may not be quite what it resembles. Tomorrow may be another song- paraphrasing a genius saint who hopefully grins as I riff a point home that may very well ring a bell in his vast collection. Deriding current geography of mind's eye which can't see home for the head it's stuck in. Can't read writing on walls anymore- not to invite cons to test their luck in straight angles of razors but something metaphysical like. Reconnoitering the landscape for a warm hearth though best I can come up with is cooling fire. Throwing pages to the wind that will never read them but perhaps sands of time might bury them for intuitive conscious of whatever it is after the future we've tossed into the chum around which the sharks circle and while having little taste for human flesh, a meal is a meal after all and tends to vary by species. Skipping any attempts at writing still-life which never pauses but for a nanosecond. Malleable expressionistic is the best I can splatter at the moment without violating the holy past her safe-words. Plundering tenets of red herrings with poisoned rice of unexpected attraction of opposite nuptials. Incalculable distance separating me from the one place I belong despite the fact we're connected at the neck and there's not a damn thing Peter Paul and Mary can belt out to alter my vomiting intoxication. Not a lemon tree sour enough. Only a hammer with which the nails are driven to evermore however I prefer a blind rendition thereof.

Numbed Down Mundane

Inescapable ennui is gaining a following in the coming twist of faithless. Grasping to nothing is actively avoiding something. Attempting an uninterruptable incorrigible collage with no boundaries outside the only mind that matters which is lost in space so there shouldn't be much trouble connecting in mid-orbit. Disinterested third party conviction is overturning the mattress yet still finding no tangible reaper types despite their shadows. Sleeping through a nap. Deciding not to decide much but everything is asking for advice- tends to send me running the other way but for a vast collection of analogous anecdotes which may only be parallel translations in my own head however keeping it under wraps is melting on the sill. Wrapping conceptual bones with a new type diction that requires no forms nor applications for entrance. Retiring to a new life which belies the term. Archaic terminology has been eternally silenced by the notes of a few explorers and couple would-be's if they cared though they refuse to attend to matters as aspiring might oblige but aspiring is no longer in the dictionary which starts at metaphysical absurdism and ends with objective water color. Discovering clarity is an opaque journey over hot coals tinged by surreal pastels. Overcooked pigs are nowhere to be found, leaving me in a room of one. Understaffed causes are muffled by the report of bamboo cane which is really beat. Scalping all inconsequential items for categorical filing to be reviewed at a future date which is albeit optimistic from my standpoint though a bit of light smacking the plotline is a non sequitur worth exorbitant sequential prices. Recasting my own illiteracy in pudding paste on intricately laid tiles is spelling out something however further enlightenment might place me on someone's bucket list and I'm trying to beat the actuaries to the punch though the cookies are following my every move and can't be deleted for some reason. It's said to be a glitch on chat boards monitored by slithering monitors from air conditioned desert perches. Boredom is a national pastime without much pull. Pressing deeper into the depression of soul is an ad suggesting piling on more obligatory notes which send greeting cards monthly- return receipt required. Slapping the baby's bottom never seemed to make sense to me though a few years changes even the kindest world view- nothing to which I lay claim. Crapping on traditional formations in order to fertilize or genetically modify a crop of up and comers which in no way is unworthy of my inclusion and successful launches into urtication fields is an underestimated career achievement. Untold damage gets a voice. Rasps of wind carry a laryngeal virus. Coughing up a hairball of life which is trauma interrupted by enough doses of elation to keep us coming back for another drip. Eternal jones for the first high with expected results- boredom in desperate withdrawal for flash-photography.

Stuck To Contemplative Couch

Never blessed with faith in an egalitarian phantom catching my back as trampolines have always been the source of the bounce which could be a transcendent concept stretching from walking dead in excrement or platinum. Inseparable codes are dancing through hydrogen populace. Striking a match in gas chambers is igniting a firestorm though the instructions are Chinese to untenable consumptive reasoning which just bought new plasma in hopes for an infusion that doesn't need be unaltered or original for that matter. Running from quantifiable earlier to unlit passages in later texts is either blinded crash into broken foundation or trip to promised land though promises are meant to be broken- especially true of deals struck in the still of stagnant murk. Uninformed positions are on a mission. Survivors are seeking asylum from temptation though organic cessation of effort is taking things into inertial insignificance by its own accord and is only a matter of time. Lonely reverie is an empty street lacking a passing lane. Inscriptions among hieroglyphics are complicating the sculpture much as direct from babes though mouths are often otherwise occupied, providing them some excuse though I've got none to rest my laurels upon however that's a moot point as garlands are scarce in these parts and rot in basement mold if left without vigilant chaperone regardless. Reaping what I sow which is still a vast ambiguity though the adjective may be a bit self-serving- regardless I still couldn't hem crooked on an even seam. Darting through ceaseless flies in the ointment is sealing scabs, allowing no airplay for wider release. Berating the only one responsible is taking breakdown of phraseology to the coroner for a more in- depth explanation on the tight lipped results unsure of subject or object in animated dissection- ergo the post mortem. Laughing off objectors before crying silent in the sandman's inconsistent job performance. Clocking in without firm scheduling is incorporating intuitive answers to questions never asked. An outline bed wonders why no queen in the California king or vice versa. Tell myself it's nothing but holistic healing in billowing cancer. Coming to grips with myself yet finding imagination poorly lacking so grab a book instead and ingest somebody else's. Denying those truths that never set one free is burning down the house. Outcast harpsichord is plucking feathers from road-kill. Pinned to the wall is a life-size impression of motivational abyss. Never thought I'd feel a touch but gave it a shot. Stepping into my indentation to avoid capture. Rewriting history which hasn't arrived using a sooty roadmap and protractor. Unseen doesn't mean it ain't there however holy water isn't sprinkling in my downpour- downgraded to occasional spurts of insight.

Assailable

Cracking the whip on inactivity is looking for another respite while stoked fireplace eats fuel. Interrupted sleep is no rest for the wicked. Repeating old saws is cutting into wood-splitting headache. Reciprocating dissociation isn't dialing. Inexorable wont for word is reading too much into the story. Skipping to the next chapter before satisfactory conclusion of previous encounters. Anticipating poor attendance to keep expectations at a minimum. Low-bars are tripping me up though concussive possibilities walk it off. Fearful simpering opinion no longer smirks at stubborn individualism armed with unassailable data points shooting down inane arguments with clarifying quips that are anything but a joke but the ignorant guffaws can't keep up the scam too discernible for even the challenged. Elixir for all ills fell off the wagon. Indigent theoretical cogitations are sleeping on subway grates. Great society is indentured servitude reeking of fascism hiding beneath claims of good will to all- who agree. Threw my back out throwing punches at a yoga instructor insisting that contortionist poses with proper breathing technique is buying the world a Coke and a smile though high-fructose has been proscribed so nobody's smiling but agricultural subsidies smoking all the way to the bank-wheezing chuckles into diesel air. There is no more snake-oil for sale but an odd concoction of organic vegetables with just a touch of this and sprinkle of that is supposedly extending lives into capitulatory hari-kari. The nanny's slapping edicts on the ass in order to get the mules running at maximum red-line. Sub and super-par achievement are rewarded with excommunication from the flat-tone compound. Chock full of dire predictions is simply graphing likely patterns of erratic flight plans whose large number belie their apathetic reactionary chaos that is entirely predictable but even paradigms of standard deviation veer off the road- create opportunity to fail standardized testing though expedience pushes them through- signs the diplomas. Hammers hone in on nail on the head but can't quite strike a vane or even ditty with an harmonic catch and release. Slapping injunctions on all unwelcome guests- three-quarters of my four corners is banned from the public house which is a return to origins though frothy mendicants are searching for an abbreviated version before sobriety rises with a belch and grease mop. Waking in alarm only to catch the buzzer before the final second expires. In time to wipe the egg off pasty bloated mug before recounting dead soldiers and sleeping dogs.

Jury Of Retrorse Peer

Unavoidable contact coming up on undesired upshots. Barking warnings while bearing unrepentant fangs. Inexcusable action precludes further contact.   Unheard music can't call off the concerto. Stepping onto to shaky foundations approaches without heed of previous testimonial.   Urging restraint is bouncing off blind rage. Minor brush with flooring too close by singular adjudication in the court of me as proscribed per above in previous edict. Ignoring penalty of law is either outlaw spirit or pig-headed which is actually an insult to swine who happen to be quite intelligent or at least that's what they tell me as I scarf their loins crispy. Counting on magnanimity is a chalk outline in a crystal ball.   Consequential altercation is deaf with rage. Ignoring calls to bring the din to a more genteel level is moving bodies to issue vengeance as it seems the lord's busy with more pressing matters.   Threats behind screen of blocking backs reignite what's coming to flame-out.   Court of me adds a contempt charge and charges. Simple narrative of simple event which occurred on a clear night beneath childhood fantasy killed off by youthful reality. Escaping to Mesopotamia on magic carpet always sounded like a decent time as long as anti-nausea patches were plentiful. Then genies I guess can always flip a twitch and make it all better. Unimpeded by the folly of the old. Fretting heir apparent title due to exorbitant rent. Would give the belt back with welts. Watch the workers toiling in angry sun while the gnats flock, air conditioned. Greener grass is cud of priority or capacity.   Unfortunate choice can be deceptive in nature or in practice mastery or execution. Tranquil is far as a vapor trail at maximum cruising altitude. Humanity dies on the floor next to the bodies. Dogs of war die young either by errant hajji jihad dressed in bed-sheet with warm hands of cold hearts or via invisible assassins. Lurkers awaiting the right moment to take the wrong guy. Reapers drooling rabid for new cardiac assessments. Peter preparing for innocent souls. Ferryman is booked. Death it appears is good business no matter how you slice it. Police action or police action- guess they cut the cake with Siamese hands of a marriage consummated in a ring of fire.

241

Wringing my hand of any collective responsibility as armed dissention is generally glowered upon in this hemisphere however new hearings are leaking war crimes into the phone-banks. And now this- a new conflict arises. Some dudes have no Seoul. Most reveries pass with fallen moons. Lone survivors hole up in secure digs. Tension snapping sleeping tendencies to life. Better to let 'em sleep. You won't like them when they wake. Always hurts me more than mindless annoyance- yeah, but it's true. Sometimes. Unblemished safety record for half decade reset. Hate starting over but time and place and heaven and all that. Retreat to linear expressions. God knows what I might fire off in the abstract. Theoretical luck shining on whomever's in the radius.

Recumbent Aggression

Not all that dissimilar is a foray into a casino or simply waking up. Unexpected upending of daydream which doesn't set with fiery orbs nor rapturous hymns in a hardened wax impression flirting with disaster at original spark however mossy ponds are splintering the brooding glass which flew me to another plane without a pilot light to prop things up. Optimistic is jumping with a chute packed by red-eyed demonic conception. Slapping eternity into a wrestling match while throwing chairs across the ring. Simmering pot is best I can muster without reinforcement or voluminous bugle. Lacking inkling of conformist data while in possession of large quantities for distribution is getting with a program lacking any steps but a hop skip and jump. Tapping out is either acquiescence to powers that be or leaving the ring before the next round is a house on the head. Lapping up veiled reference is sandpaper with pointed terms and conditions floating in dander through wisps of dancing poison in the moonlight. Unexplored entry points are safe from incursion though they always catch you where unexpected. Stuck to my coat-tails is a ring-tailed lemur and eight hundred pound gorilla which is less concern than the former as the ape sits patiently for my collapse before unleashing rage. Estimated longevity calculation was biggest concern though fairly confident I won't be around when the silverback goes belly-up which may obviate the need to get that monkey off my back. Seeping with thoughts that can't find their way to the navigation system. Schisms of sharpened stakes taking part in a cover-up with palm fronds and twigs. Next chapter is a fifty-fifty shot no matter how many times it's come up red. Unspoken word isn't negotiating. Untilted pinball wizard isn't scratching the table. Fabric is unwoven at hope and dream alley. Goal is a four letter word or trip down under. Karmic solutions seem the safest bet if mystic incantations are ringing clear. Spitting goodwill into the wind if only to test boomerang theory. All I hear are hisses sounding like a scathing attack on anything objective which is relative to functionality of quality control. Nobody's superstitious outside a gambling hall. A bus stepped in front of me this morning. Take the pass-line downtown and keep going through the misty night into a world of my own making which has nothing whatsoever to do with anything I accomplish though luck is a double edged sword which grabs your chips at the first intersection of chance and too tired to drive with a spicy chaser indifferent to plight of odds. Unsympathetic towards walking wounded wound too tightly around tomorrow while today has yet to fully unleash its ration of terror.

Ruff Start

"the more i know about people,
the more i like my dogs."

~mark twain

Engaged at maintaining autonomy via divorce from the race though ground-rules won't allow secession despite refractory patches of honed briar beds laid at their feet in midnight musings when the hills are howling dogs gnawing on wayward housecat caught without papers. Enmity is an up and comer on the commodity desk. Flipping manual disbelief to elude the camera angle showing my bad side which is an allusion to the side that disagrees with everything that makes you tick. It's in your blood so we'll have to check to make sure. Lab rats running labyrinths into blocks of cheese which shrunk since last year. Social interaction is of questionable discretion as prior restraint has been lifted and the psychos are on the loose. Denting the vellum on many layers is hooligan humanistic impression leaving fossilized evidence of sage warnings which any idiot could have figured out with a slide-rule and abacus however intuitive inclinations are scowled upon while they tell you to trust your gut- an irreconcilable detail which is more than a stick in the spokes which now snap so loudly even Switzerland activates troops. Indelible prints on women and children selected for the great suffering while the gods sleep and the devil's workshop is running three shifts and still can't gear up sufficiently to handle the workload. Meds distributed slow-hand. Insane throw bricks at a jailhouse. Sahara is laughing hyenas resting in oasis shade while prey scavenge refuse hills for scraps. Blood trails lead from everywhere to here. Mobs rule the street ruled by the local authorities- masterwork collusion with federal inefficiency which carries a sentence of higher office until the nose-bleed hits the wires and Google image gallery. The cops are here to help you- to a hospital so long as the beat is worth the typing. Zealots are preaching hate as the faithless struggle for their existential romp through indefinable battle scars. Fishy story isn't catching on but then you can fool most of the people most of the time is a gaping equivocation. Remarkable inhumanity isn't noteworthy for its verb which is a constant if not definitive but for the fact anyone would find it worthy of attention. The flag of smiley happy ignorant foolish half-witted dim-witted subsea sludge disseminator is leaving a foul stench in a preempted primetime slot and the almighty is brought to the Lazy-Boys so as not to lose attention during limited commercial interruptions. Braining my skull all over the abrasive texture seems to get nowhere but makes for a decent carnival side-gig. Sweating for answers on subhuman condition needs not to leave his loft unattended. Can just but watch as poker-faces, which once the bluff is exposed to the elements chip away at the stone until it is bland in an hourglass or another day in the life- don't read the news for its redundant thematic attributes- it ain't ending better than highball or sloe gin. Running out of quasi cliché pop-reference from dead suns. Looking back on why it is I gave any a chance in the first place. Nothing deflates more than a relationship in throes of truthful discourse or telling lack thereof. Attempting an epic of my inane epoch is running short on time. Fatal design is flawed planning or blessing in disguise. Not to say profundity is coursing my veins like a warm piercing though blind squirrels and nuts sums it up. Thin is the span between love and hate. Is predisposition denied its predilection. Tribal warfare wished away on the back of magic Hindi whose texts don't read well is distinct only for the pop-ups between the pages which are like a mobile above my crib and can't soothe the rage that is inclusionary conscription- born into a band of fools who never crack the charts. Fools come in numbers from missions about the globe though hush money usually keeps the rugs from getting the beaten vetting they've rightfully earned in earnest though I'm certain they could have without him too. Consumer reports deplorable creatures are invariably bipodal though rarely trustworthy is anything anybody says yet the dagger in the kidney is making me a believer. Perhaps not the kind kind. From the uterus of humanity's sins against persons, births a misanthrope. Dude's gotta start somewhere. Might as well be zero.

Riotous Script

Spinners are flipping out of wavelength merriments in protest of working conditions and demands for reparations. Can't stand on two feet but can lug a liberated big-screen from any riot scene- sofa from which to rejoice in tow with progeny who never know any better but to follow footsteps straight to the hoosegow which is now banished to Australia- clanking chains and all. Set free to destroy is another in myriad screw-ups in the first draft selectively redacted in future additions without regard to sobbing savior who dropped for someone's sin that wasn't mine however means don't justify ends so I'll take it with a grain of salt in the lashes. Swallowing my tongue to avoid choking on my words. Inescapable isn't a blanket statement but for those freezing in empty souls of entitled class which recognizes no boundary nor safety net which might lead one to confuse me with class warrior though I won't honor the deathly misinformed with a response. Casting vilifications on all responsible stands me in a corner with gummy aroma but I can't hum a different tune. Skedaddling to disparate notions because that's how the brain works seems as good an explanation of the expressionistic hedonism practiced till fingers bleed onto a drenched rug which never takes flight. Rapping inconsistent is pulling the strings together but the marionette is still tangled at the source. Fairness is a fable no longer in the broad vernacular due to its own pompous semantic dislocation from a history which never allotted much time and space to utter nonsense. Recapping events with a wooden steed is no longer necessary as the wells have been topped off with explosive charges sent to scuttle the blackened sky- something of potentially ironic implications though irony is a paradox that always escapes on a mockery. Installing cataracts to minimize sight-distance or risk suffering fools who I must admit have suffered me plenty but then nobody lays claim to rich soil or infertile cogitation which go anywhere but where they were intended at conceptualization in form of a single line that spawns headstrong apples falling from the bastard tree with a chip on their shoulders. Degradation to retrograde is playing mind tricks on the heart.

Throwing a wide net to capture butterflies released from the cocoon into the entropy that's the attic of one plus or minus a coupla bats. God rest their souls should they fall in the clutches of guano before fruition. Looking for a superhero yet they fall from reels fast as they're exploited for maximum box-office- best I can do is a weak Sam Jackson impression on a set of Corman's tits or in the pulp of resurrection scraping from a video geek's worn sneakers.

Generation What?

Impenetrable defensive measures on the lam from authorities unwittingly indifferent towards the security breach. Hounded by canines which refuse to bite the tongue in evasive fashion leading to unsealing of records that should have been buried in the dunes blanketed in lye or fed to the pigs. Cancelling any planned excursions into twilight of delusional flame-throwers not part of my cause which begins and ends with whatever it is I find most appealing in the discourse which is typically anathema to the chosen speakers though amplified at high levels is just asking for excommunicative action. No skin off my teeth which have already lost their enamel in previous showdowns and rest on ambivalent gums of solid roots notwithstanding signs of a grind exceeding warrantied protection. Dagger quill is slicing up the sword yet it would be a substantive overstatement to claim disavowal of incumbent armed conflict. Matching wits with humorless is a game show with no consolation outside the green room which is turning pale sea-foam. Lost in a missing generation which screams from papal heights while I rest on an altar of post-revelatory disinherited. Willing obligatory inertia on perpetually languid is futile enterprise though value is in the effort if one is to label conscription a cornerstone of let us bleed. Compromised principles are fighting for dear life so as not to fall another rung into concession within a faithful psyche which believes in nothing though degenerative negotiating positions are missions of fending off broadside dogma from weakened standing of too many years under its autodidact belt- somewhere between withering bullhorn and virulent .45, refusing middle ground because it implies giving in. Something short of nihilistic is reexamining uncertain tumors. Locked away of sorts in what might as well be primordial genetic misstep is sipping nectar and detritus through a perforated straw. Broken camel is too easy so will just say I never got a good hump in the wilderness. Seeing red while looking into faces painted in rocks which hold all the secrets in phantom mineral formulations we're implored to ingest while we sail further into why bother draining to colostomy bags and vocal incontinence. Beautiful is a sunset with no interruptive sound bytes taunting my cadence though lonely backbeats are slowly taking their toll. Unappreciated breaths are exalted when peering over the fence. Writing a believable end to inanity in search of meaning where life stings arrhythmic patterns without letting on who's next but the certainty is assured- any suggestions to the contrary are hung by elevated cables high on liquid somnambulism. Mirror image deleting connections in a snow drift that smells like white-out though never runs when confronted with popular opinion. Which avoids contact to close the book and move forward violating a no-contact order with utopia though the latter's number is unlisted anyway and the messiahs thereof can't get a valid thought in edgewise but sure have firm ideals as to methodical evisceration of dissent for the sake of single-minded determination to off all rats in the cellar. Even those from superior institutions of learning- jungles of concrete lacking a single strand of ivy or spare room for the last remaining hater-currently throwing the scent off the trail via multitude misdirects backed by the full faith and credit of over the limit debt facilities. Redoubled effort at avoiding the cauldron of witches in gingerbread forests which can't see themselves for the fuel in the mirror.

Borderline Mania With Dubious Adjective

Denied ample opportunity to slip through cracks in the sidewalk to avoid scorning elements and enlightening street lamps wishing nothing except pointing out my deficiencies. Mirror in the bathroom can accomplish the same thing or provide a foundation for temporary euphoria- latter drips sending copper to the scrap pile for remunerative purposes but instead seizes the day. Renewed examination of spirit is thinking through the testing standards. Irregular visits with apnea are snorting puffs of a magic dragon though odor of sulfur remains notwithstanding the brevity. Grappling with a Brazilian is choked out or smooth landing strip. Planes dropping from the skies like collisions in Koreatown. Blinded with dental floss is unfortunate attribute when operating heavy machinery though the label says nothing about caution. Holes in the roof are axed to relieve pressure allowing for swift exit of phantom explanations. Unemployment checks are peeking in on operational inconsistency though documents are either forged or brazenly distributed to the naked eye which has only a toothpick between it and tranquil conscience. Leaping to conclusions has landed on woeful which is a don't pass go type solicitation. Shooting for Coltrane yet finding nothing but hot-air occasionally accompanied by a small acorn which is quickly devoured by nuts which that are only half the story. Painting Pollock though still can't dissect one drop from another. Drool-cup fully in place would be a wise addition to the wardrobe however might invite sympathy or at least empathetic doe-eyed hospitality- something I turn on its head after spitting on so many tails. Actively begging for maintenance of tranquil as the gentle sway of a palm frond under a marine layer breeze however the ravens are circling a bond with rapacious kamikazes. Generalized penance isn't pestilence avoided though perhaps extends the manufacturer's return policy. Leaking new information is coming out in the wash. Laying down a gauntlet to accept whole kit and caboodle or nothing at all has few takers yet the offer remains open for bookworms or super models so long as they leave in the mourning. Replacing beating hearts with defibrillators to save on electric bills. Trickling into shadow which will have to do as the aerie has begun talking to me-admittedly a possible doppelganger admonishing me for behavior which punishes none though retrorse deviations take a toll on everybody surrounding radius despite they're more the norm than deviant in the transmutative sense of the word which I'm probably murdering in execution of the point. Regard external missives with no praise. Exalting rutted walkways and shot-out illumination during darkest hours. Keeping opaque front and center until I can find either. Lurid erections of corpus-delecti which has yet to pass the borders promising lascivious encounters with nirvana. Promises in the dark are fibs in the light. Safer in sobs than taking slices of lobes so far the cat-scan can't make rhyme or riddle of Polaroid nor digital remaster. Farther than the collection of dreams upon which I lay wreaths with every respiration.

Alienated

"...so why do they make me stand in front
of class of gawking fools who'll never understand?"

~ *adolescents*
tell me who is who

It's come to this- overactive limbic system singing the blues in pubescent minor. Old habits die wondering. Caving into a complete separation of church of one and state of all. Conception to eternity. Absurdity to nowhere cuz it's got nowhere to go. No hiding places sufficiently ashen as to conceal fundamental reality. Strapped to a seat holding no mercy between paranoia and intuition which has never steered me wrong though I've often veered off prescribed headings into predictable cinder displaying a lack of adherence to the infallible strategy but for the critical juncture- manned by fallible creature. Collapsing under weight of circumstance and choice some may call fortunate. Begging their presence in me, this antipodal dissonance of galactic proportions with too many scratches to forgive the impaling of self for which the demon laughs while the angel sobs yet sometimes immutable natural balance must revert to the mean and sometimes the mean ain't too friendly- but digressing, get no takers. Kind isn't a cornerstone of either natural nor by extension, social convention- itself a maddening collection of horseshit- social that is- compiled, artificial balm for flesh wounds burned into psyches via repetitive passing of the sacrificial guilt- denomination neutral. Schoolyard antics turn a blind eye to the lonely kid in the corner unable to shut the nest where the crows roost and rarely recant well received tales. If only to shut the system down for maintenance. If but to recreate the code- work out the bugs. The ice could melt certainly but the tropics are overrated and Florida could use a cleanse regardless. A funny bone refuses to laugh in the toxic vibe permeating the rhythm of the day- actually plural but artistic license applies to diatribes much as supposed literature of questionable alias that defiles the canon however that much can be tolerated if for no other reason than tradition needs a kick in the ass if history's any guide which is most certainly a redundancy in the scope of my meanderings yet always worthy of repetition as it tends to repeat while we pretend not to notice in favor of digging the zeitgeist for the sake of communal confirmation of status among domestic war mongers looking to incorporate their hate into a love of man type script and are actually attracting corporate interest- a buck after all...won't cover Michael Moore's appetizer but it's still a buck... At the point of complete severing of all ties to the outside world which sometimes should blow itself off the map though self-fulfilling prophecies need not be repeated barring some sort of Rip Van Winkle type thing in your hindsight or lack thereof. Dripping with too much knowledge is a dry faucet. A spigot incapable of holding back its sarcastic overtones with a strong undertow of loathing pulling closer to the sea-bed with each dish of salt projectile spat at the walking waste surrounding my every move. Lost intuition from earlier in the rants of a paradoxically madly sane-madman is reappearing in chaotic form as the mind is wont- knows what's up with what but will never hear what's new from the whispers of poetic court any more than court of law, coterie of hypothetically friendly spirits or public outcry. Congenial is too close for comfort with deeply flawed format if dissected with explicit larceny of heart. Might this close the chapter? Descending ever more stairs into what appears to be a shrinking room without portal though the stripes throw off an affect that can't be understood without interpretation. Progressive arguments for peace are demands for strict compliance. Bitter group of self-endowed counter-culture formers currents and never-were nor will-be's crashing egos off each other's self importance. Impossible to catch a groove with thinly veiled hip has fully stacked the odds- ain't looking much better than conclusions drawn and quartered on the bodies of apparitional friends choking on dust of deflated value. Wishing on a star is plucking an eyebrow and blowing it to the upwind in vain hopes that it doesn't come back to alter vision in the future- the innocence of youth in adults who should know better. Decry my name around a gas pyre while the steam rises from your infected nostrils. I'm gonna nap any remaining trust from a hopeless arrangement. When I awake- you'll be gone. Creations of my own mind leveled like a double-wide in a tornado. Always know who's coming if nobody's coming. Intentions are immaterial without contact. Sinatra singing of summer winds- who the fuck was he kidding or did we just come from different planets? What was that platform of conformity again? Not that it matters- your names have been deleted. Unfortunately your recreation won't smell much differently than your chum if laws of large numbers hold true after the insurrection so I'll be more deliberate or at least attempt to negate your rebirth with all due chants in seven distinct chapels none of which points to Mecca though lately I haven't been assaulted by a single Arab- none toot towards Salt Lake either- so keep your camel spit while I equivocate- don't look a gift hump in the mouth. Friends call me enemy- enemies, friends. Agoraphobia ponders in its alone-time. Lament to interpersonal contact is mourning loss of what never was while Dixieland can only manage a mixed message. Maybe we all need name tags- the numbers are starting to itch.

Reconciling Bleat Goes On

Disregarding objective logic for ideational is rethinking philosophical underscores to find lowest common denominator in quest for the missing link or at least flexible hypothesis. Rapping it out like Compton without backbeat nor cop-killing while keeping with the canons I devised for myself though missing synaptic cleft is close-lipped on the study. Ingratiating is ruining art via maudlin sycophantic supplication however open palms make for good ashtrays- not much else. Slapping an enjoiner upon all banished hysteria is losing patience with the system. Cross words are reorganizing amid a union vote. Lacking direction is a stream with a definitive path in mind. Hyping up on misplaced cogitations is working in tandem with intellectual variations creating what appears contrary but is only so due to like-charged electrons going to neutral corners between rounds of raving inconsistency and uncontrollable urge. Connecting with the world at large is shrink wrapped though noticeably gaining weight. Tilting to a new world view in expression of what changes from moment to moment while the attic sits unattended and a breeze flowing through the prancing curtains brushes by horded antiquities before whisking off to fictional yarns. Scrapping old plans for new is being interrupted by ignorant powers looking for companionship but I can't be a friend to everyone- especially those dragging me back to calcified timeline that should be leveled like a crack-house. Two bit peddlers of nonsense are beginning to close in on a sale yet in every way possible I just turn the other cheek to a more subtle pomposity stinking of the queen's English which doesn't fit my esthetic so switching back to duct-taped sound blinded by the light of well positioned expletive. Dashing between nothing important and it can wait is a slash mark on a calendar with no schedule. Apple-pie is pregnant but barely into the first trimester so it's still hush-hush and will likely be aborted but forward movement is pissing off the status quo desiring nothing but homesteads and distance from those who'd deny property rights while certifiably crossing live-fire signs without prior notice delivered- registered by a money losing psych-ward-statutorily drafted to be shedding accounts. Try that blinds is match-making true-life saga with expanding boundaries. Sculpture carved is voice heard. All of them- even if from the bowels of dissent escorted from the chamber in unmistakable jumpsuit which is leaping to conclusion of all things possible. And a few not though it's not mine to question the usual suspects. They always have matching alibis anyway- show up the same time in the same clothes and pile more paperclips to be shuffled.

On A Plane

Incapacitated skill may be a temporary fracture or simply speaking its mind without admitting so much in absence of deep byline clouding the whole story. Virtuous attempts at reparations are met with immoral condemnations by the voice that counts failure as bully pulpit. I've a pain in the belly which won't quit. Medicating out of situational awareness is putting me to sleep but can't quite break the cycle of apocalyptic anecdotal interjection into optimistic countenance that loses face upon discovery or final awakening which is apparently only a journey or that's what they say to keep us in line when the phoenix is otherwise occupied. Non-aggression pact between bland narrative and rich impression is on the verge of signing on the highlights but still has some wrinkles to iron out. Elusive gist is getting in the way of the synopsis though won't give in to demands of hijacked success. Putting a dollop of pesticide on malignant growth atop benign tumors to achieve unabashed pride which is equivocating on the epistemology of shame. Making it on a wing and a dare from mother superior who should know better than to drop the hammer or issue a challenge is struggling up the little engine that could type hill and still doesn't know if it can. Trudging along in fortunate misfortune can't declare a winner and the belt is whipped out for cut down the middle ground that can't find a midpoint on the arc from parabola to grave. Anything but seamless transition is hemmed into serrated schemes that look nothing like the perfect mannequin display which is checkering at critical juncture. Unavailable subject matter is sought after employee that can't be distracted by outside influences however drought obliges tackling the job with heavy test line. Snap judgments are pressing into organic shallots despite pleas for additional preparative allowances. Day is coming unless I will it not to in which case I'll be staying in for the foreseeable future. Citing multiple sources in the footnotes are captions which may as well be primordial fossils. Crystalized outbursts are shattering the linoleum. Floored by recent acceleration of the process is throwing question marks at reliable sources which are typically parties of one- exclusive of indiscernible riled chipping cicadas which extinguish smoking guns before I can find the pedestal upon which they preach- negating purpose of the din- perhaps precisely the point of their mockery or cautionary tales- potentially portentous warnings- whichever the case may be. Third party accounting of conditions from first person perspective on the look-out for another county heard from. Hopefully it won't be LA. Love affair with redundancy has its limits.

Progress Deconstructed

The cold ground ate the blustery nights frozen in duality of autonomy. Where evil lurks from every fissure in the foundation of the edifice which is the decline of all civilizations. Reaping quarry is in the mezzanine- orchestra playing silent-movie danger- fugue. Tectonic plates cracking at the edges. Quaking federalists shivering in the heat. Lapdog endpoints to game of charades lasting too long for completion though unspoken conclusion points to a mastodon in the rubber-room whose clanking foyer is jabbering gibberish to the smash of martinis. Lapsing into temporary sense of adrift though sitting in familiar digs. Train of thought is losing cars at every turn. They slide down archaic tracks into an eon's trough of a long-lost anecdote which rarely fits the landscape. External stimulus comes machine gun staccato- throws brass into the wind while the bats dance in the rain- disconnected but for impressions drunk on their own blur. The boxcars back into scooting from yard to loft in the sky- free but for the risk of rusted fire escapes or deliberation of intent which places a spotlight on events. Starlit boulevard bustles foreboding- victim of manifest destiny choking on its own conclusion- whose shine had long since been worn into a magnificent testament to rogues and pimps and whores and pierced emancipated teens and sizzling rock and gangsters among slobbering chicken-hawks and greasy pizza- all stirring in unseemly yet oddly sweet broth not yet cooled into child-safe velvet rope hipster fuckface. Not yet into clean and tidy reversal of misfortune which had already once defiled her marred elegance. Hiding in the shadows are around the corner. Holed up in motel rooms uncharted by AAA or AA. They're waiting for your stitches to come undone-staples removed with rabid fangs. Counting the seconds until a slip up falls all over itself and nothing in the magic bag of tricks can prevent viral interaction over the ether or liberated Nikon. And fools disguised as stars are born- as more alluring shine diminishes- former clearly more relevant to exigent circumstance as we won't know of the latter until long after we'll be knowing anything. Expired celestials illuminating the blatant incivility of the most civilized ticks on the clock or overdoses after too much ingestion of self. Heads- I win with like implication on diametric flip-side. Digging that idea so I'm endeavoring to come up with more sure-fire manners by which to dupe someone other than myself into assisting in the plot which was lost five floors above the menacing. On a roof in clutches of petrifying freedom so intoxicating as to erect a flag. Forty ounces washing microdots gurgling with wiggling holographic propensities. Notoriety is novelty- kitsch adorning trinkets where we stood watch in strictly undefined formations. Red carpets and grand auditoriums cover the bones of a dilapidated structure once providing those cracks for the malfeasant to occupy in shiver. Relegated to side-streets where clearing the decay is less a priority until a neighbor complains. Where even once forbidding alleys are no longer roads less traveled. Rusted spikes and termite ties breathing paradox harmony with new and approved maximum density.

Hall Of Blame

Putting recent events into box-score format is providing the scouts with hybrid sentiment which doesn't bode too well for future negotiations but it could be worse. Underlying thesis is being tested though the monkeys have been let loose while under the influence of stimulative formulas that cause the last remaining to fall into deep depression. The toads are groaning while the alligators croak. Denying genetic miscues for more enlightened approach is requesting a duel at twenty paces though can only fire off so many wheat-free platitudes before erudite logic sends them back in a fireball of immolated model inanity cracked from incipient conception of no umbilical unification. Skimming the surface is missing character development. Inscrutable demands on resourceful casks is draining blood through a fermented spigot- silent but for the unheard screams beneath acerb of mad genius hiding his concotion like an ancient Chinese secret with too much starch. Falling to pieces is earning runs on the bank though what goes in comes out in the end. Borderline personality disorder is stuck between bifurcation and braggadocio. Trending in downward sloping hyperbole is false modesty with too much feigned humility abutting an ego on sabbatical. Disenfranchised disconnect is worlds apart- soup cans lacking sufficient twine to pull it all together. Tossing out the first pitch is a veteran balk which goes unnoticed until batter up can't rise to the occasion and rolls over on accomplices however could just as easily be a quick exit. Recanting unbecoming tales of factual yarn slumped together with fictional events is keeping performance enhancing drugs out of the hall so I'll never get admitted but for a potential competency hearing to examine the capacity of whomever's listening which won't do me much good but I've been promised ice-cream and a hot dog if I cooperate. Chilling after-effects are leaving men off base though crass can have that influence on people and unbalanced tap-dance is a one punch knockout in a pinch when cheeky sots with distended gums and bulbous noses refuse conflict resolution. Incapable of quantification is beginning to get a good head count. Field stripped of turf is rocks in the head or too much information leaked in pop-up children's books despite viewer discretion advised. Riding the white bull in a china shop is nauseating the crowd during the seventh-inning stretch. Preferring chance for an explosive dirigible cannot by definition be good and rich but perhaps expansive nature of balloons will keep the stats on the up and up and maybe keep the career in motion longer than anticipated. Unsure whether a blessing in disguise or curse implanting stitches into a photograph which never catches the good side but captures eyes well enough to see the screams.

The Price

Intensity is rising- not a goddamn thing I can do about it. Nightfall security blanket is easily unstrung like the notes weeping desperate fair-wells. Stone ovens form respite caves for superior creatures who add hisses to a pentatonic scale- demanding a recount- clear warning of rockslides but we stick our hands in cracks anyway. In a different climate zone without moving a muscle. Stovepipes have a six octave range and limitless variations on taking the heat. Red lines ex'ing out a circular of ego denying its own press while the faces crumble under their own sensation. Battling for reparations is slow a boat to nobody knows the heading which is pointing south and looks to have some tortillas in the pan. Conflicting sign language rules the streets however most seem easy aside from minor nuance of translating public wasted on too much or forgotten on not enough. Kin to diamond/water paradox mentioned previously but the lineup specifies substitution of top shelf and fortification. Wrestling with indulgent sense of self while jerking to a sudden stop at lost imagery. Counting rings after volunteering for slicing commentary of a prop comic is missing a finger. Watching the turkey-vultures gnaw on the last man standing from a lounge chair on a tor situated in prime spot for open and unchecked polemics is easy on the lower back which is breaking from the heft of straw dogs which should be weightless. Taking the high ground can be a lull in Darwinian demands. Shady binoculars are acting suspicious. Frying an egg with expulsion of electrical excess. The Joshua trees dance in premeditated celebration- know it will soon be theirs that get wetted without commercial interruption or Winnebago warriors who can't be blamed for wanderlust though the black socks have to go. Lasting well beyond the longest shot on the board doesn't recognize the last roll but can't contain inevitable backlash. Persistent reference to games of chance have been on the agenda since MGM took over management. My friend carries the jawbone of an ass with which he'd bring down the steeples but sharpening bone for mission-specific purposes is a bit dicey. Can't escape what won't reveal itself yet can't reveal what won't escape. Forgotten cheat sheet is losing grade but time marches to the beat of a different drum machine. Entreating a way out but the world keeps shrinking- exit doors occluded. Man in a crate lacking a one-inch punch struggling for air in the monoxide orbit. Wrestling demons while trying to appease the angels before they defect to an upended ballast. Laughing off condemnation before crying myself to sleep which I never do but on occasion when it becomes apparent that death isn't a logical conclusion but entirely rational and the non-negotiable price of admission at that.

Mirrored Regression

"i only wanted to find out what sort of man you are, for so many unscrupulous people have got hold of the progressive cause of late and have so distorted in their own interests everything they touched, that the whole cause has been dragged in the mire."

~dostoyevsky
crime and punishment

Gyratory tumult- redundancy slipping into offensive diatribe of wicked intent attempts to silence repetition which struts proud its mangled combinations held over rote tradition. Centrifugal allegiances begin spinning backward- tossing the baby with the bath water but it was a filthy bastard anyway so screw the outcome of which we'll never know but for extrapolation of the model out to manifest destiny or at a minimum revolting conclusion. Chaos is taking orders and dishing 'em out with ferocious vigor. Landscapes have morphed into a melting watercolor of black and white though I'm told those aren't by definition colors but shades of grey areas. Scalping the controls for a bit of skin is falling on its belly. Reprimanded opposition to truth born of the fruit of thy womb Darwin is shopping for non-denominational votive candles and iconic symbols of bodhisattva however sculpture is subject to interpretation and an enlightened stick figure would suffice just fine. Battling for supremacy are diametrically antagonistic fictitious allies stabbing each other in the back until the front turns to common foreign enemy though rules of engagement are murky and wrought with laconic instructions shedding no light on situational awareness so the daggers turn to any port out of form. Camping out at the organic pesticide stand- wondering how much it costs to spray an organic but am refused service as the air of upcoming beef is causing a stink. Watching as they scurry to their next séance seeking wisdom of Whitman yet they only catch flash-shots of CNN. Usurped basis for existence is awol though suspected to be hiding in plain sight of an elephant type god or Gaia. Lashing out at infidels like a hajji with a cause and the redundancies go filing on. Casting spells of witches brew upon unknown ethos while depleting the world its granola resource. Barbaric infighting is making for great communal photo despite the graphic illustration of a thousand words. Of man unaltered. Can't stomach two is forming an alliance of a hundred thousand just to make a point upon which the bipartisan committee couldn't agree, so reinforcements had to be called in to simplify the irony or just practice insincere quasi-mystic clique hugs before anyone feels the break. Ruptured bones of hollow movement brought to bear by the ugliest of all free roaming spirits on her face. Writing their own dirges in the kindest possible terms- rich in texture of the good deeds to which they lay claim while free-press is slapping a high price on individuals and laying out group discounts like drunken prom queens notwithstanding indefinable quantity of the movement which seeks a constitutional audience as it deprives the first chapter its sacred air. Notwithstanding unforgivable breaking of the only canon that matters. Notwithstanding a run on oxygen bars and lemon grass. Plinking at the low lying fruits while powers that be hide in their reflection however I'm having trouble making the distinction.

Reaction

Manipulative support beams proving gender specific prowess. Pining for distant fjord or at least a cabin in the woods where solipsistic hallucinations kick detritus out for broken bonds are simply too many cracks in the head. Can take art from the gallery but not gallery from the art- laying with dogs needs a flea dip. Infested shield refusing to unravel wound too tight puts on a good show for blowing the outside world. Tail wind is a closed truck door racing from the terminal in fever pitch-throwing me to reinforced walls of questions never to receive honest response and antipathetic ambivalence which sheds layers without substantial sleeping aids or accompanying diagram though the port may have already been closed for routine maintenance. Fuck me once and I'll fuck myself for the balance of existence until I jettison your memory into airborne pathogen which is likely beyond plausibility but the medicine cabinet is full and keys are tapping all your banks into a broken levee which drowns passersby in frothy boulders and stumps with too many branches to count. Repetitive miscue is tattooed across sunburnt forehead like a gang sign dripping tears some might mistake for caught bodies but in fact are only a creation of latchkey lonesome dove with a spine broken thrice on another day in paradise which isn't all it's cracked up to be. Supplanting any and all attempts at picking a white lotus which will always turn rancid is acceptance of fate that some think of as pessimistic though I prefer more honest discourse. Contorting narrative into biographical accounts can't bend the story long enough to bleach the blood and omission under purple lights refracting in shattered faith. Undeniable superstition raises a list of interrogatories in hearts and minds of those who possess either but that fate's been sealed as null and void in forty nine states plus fugue which has been raised from the dead to most wanted listing with pill bottle forwarding address. Puking tears into a mason jar for future consideration while avoiding contact with anything that might take on the simulacra of warm. Updrafts are preparing a proposal with no wings to glide upon their furious gusts. Singing birds delivered were supposedly doves but virginal paint wears quickly in salt air and the pigeons silently bid a final adieux while storing the subterfuge in unspoken detail. Taking all I ever needed on a trip to a fiery river but physical limitations prevent swimming the schism so I'll have to pay the captain for the crossing however I refuse nailed to a cross once again as it's becoming habitual and I swore no oath to impoverished psyche yet actions speaking in shrill insinuations appear to belie that declaration despite that selfless foot massages aren't part of my depraved esthetic. A pang in the gut is the destination of divine laughter of which I'm fully deserving. Canning aspiration for something down to earth is too much gravity however is the better of two evils. Wish I could figure which is which. Picking a winner from icy steam in eighty five degree coordinates. Saving me from my own before the voices no longer escape but engage in chemical romance which always overdoses. At least that's what myself tells myself as no good deed goes unpunished hides under bland etiquette that sends thank you notes for spurious purpose which didn't catch the flaming bus to sincere. Instead pulls the buzzer for egress from the handcuffs taking me straight down- an act of compassion sorely missing its latter syllables. Lesson of what not to do is lost on never been there. Staring at inked musing representing every failure- all of which have my fingerprint lifted by forensic analysts- all petrified by the looping commentary. Terrified by its hermetic implication which might one day bare its fangs outside the cage constructed to protect earth her violators that is the sum total of the problem in the first place. Erection non-extant unless I hoist the flag of allegory and compare my span in order to gain comprehension of the four ton gorilla in the island mist.

Next

Truncated breaths suffocating under key and a lock resting upon a bed with incongruent outlines. What passes for grand illusion is redirecting traffic to take what you get and be happy. Don't worry. They're here to soothe all the wounds with Hindu shim-sham and pure meals which drip undisclosed pesticide. Just another issue in a string measuring from here to jungle canopy which can be confused for doppelgangers however could be deemed as far off point. What sufficed for innocuous rhapsody of setting sun is now foremost consideration, for uncompleted works are wasted beginnings. Common denominator is another way of admission of guilt though I prefer to render my own decisions as the courts seem too lenient for the judgmental portion of my triad to accept a plea deal. Capturing any glimpse of hope is squinting towards the end-zone behind reflective glass so nobody sees the emotional descension falling from an oily hotplate into a vat of gestating bio-fuels. Relational claims inconsistent with ideal are sitting alone with coffee and cancer. Counterpoint however is too painful to bear. Creases working overtime reconciliation shifts are straining for fruition though can't find resolution in the concerto. A lithe understudy is filling for the fat lady once again consuming processed diabetes as a promotion for a great hostess who begged her assistance for a lifetime supply. Detracting elements are subtracting today. Unessential adornments stand before the firing squad or outgoing postbox- marked no returns accepted but an acidic repeat performance is back due to popular demands of dastardly motive of which I've yet to have clue but my throat is burning with desire for the scoop. Inexcusable spontaneous combustion is predictable as old faithful. Spearing anything that comes by for tactile indiscretion shows no deliberation in sleeping arrangements which tends to upset the entropy. Avoiding endorsement like the human plague. Pestilent bacteria chewing original substance into distilled echoes- diluted so as not to interfere with acrimonious tidings making the art or operating the loom. Deep in summer of discontent following a phantom phase of clarity. Turbulent remediation attempts continue constriction of the thorax but don't finish the job. Nobody gets off that easy. Riding shortwaves to jagged sand is rolled like a ragdoll though comes up standing on crippled inspection reports when full fledged pile drive would have made midnight that much easier to swallow. Fear and hate seeking a new son. Someone who plays well with others regardless of diminished returns assuming there was anything but absolute value in the first place. Further confusing the crowd of one though contextual guidance is abundantly illuminative as to which side of zero do the numbers lie.

Coffee In Hell

I sit where an abortion that didn't take took protect and serve to a whole new level. I sit where a rescued family still dances in the ephemera of yesterday. Where the one I chased away sipped hot-chocolate as the infernal unquantifiable masses passed towards the sand and boardwalk while my salvation was released for her best interests- promising gems need not be turned jade when a diamond needs but a few months to birth. Inescapable data is a rap sheet held front and center by spindly fingers which neither forgive nor forget to remind you of their presence. Hypothetical entanglements with machinations of trading soul for brilliance already gave away the store and are left with bare shelves to offer in return despite unreciprocated promise. New blood might stoke the embers so they may once again find the flames hopefully not encircled by a quasi-hippy fest beating bongos of love to the bang of all's fair in love and war. Inaccurate boomerang loathe is starting to find its mark. Unwitting rube for supine handed charlatans with unsound overflow valves. Dejected deportment is carrying on a blue-face tantrum- out of sight out of mind. Rampaging protestors stuck in a mosquito net receiving few nibbles. Piles of buried waste product are spewing white methane over the hills which left dales out of the credits due to collective ignorance of the definition. More distressing than Aqualung in a schoolyard is a cold draining nostril on the fallacy of whatever makes one tick. Scientific method is convinced the bigger they are the harder they tumble however size is a relative matter. Bulging pockets are a hard rain gonna fall flat on cleft windshields and polluted wells. Distress signals are flaring up yet remain unseen due to unfortunate longitude. Scabbing old wounds was healing until metastasis tore into fresh flesh-eating virus trooping double-time through the core- tasting none of the apple due to excessive haste and advanced medical technique- pissing nature off to the point of a stronger dosage of plague to which the researchers can't render immunity. Stinging tears represent unforeseen events. Loyalty assumed is a bar below even previous dire estimates which took a rough spill on ungrounded concrete.

Creaks in the night are singed photos in rapid succession. Tearful supplication is delivered hot coals. Consistently poor choice is recurring to the verge of renewed dislocation seeking permanent residence while tossing no stabs in the dark. Streaking lower in the sailing winds implicative of a delayed flight out. Not bidden but for a three party event to which I received no invitation. Inexcusable missteps upon my own soul. The Stranger never cared. Raskolnikov, too much. All will die. Some sooner than others. But then Camus postdated Dostoyevsky which might have changed things if thrown in reverse. I ponder whether even the properly exalted latter could have been immune to the former. Would Raskolnikov's treetop still have sweated the small stuff? Will mine ever stop or am I simply underestimating weight in a premature bow to certain? Animated still-born remains before me as I sip bruised inspiration. Missed opportunities attach to the beach-bound in a thousand points of blown filaments.

Held In Contempt

Too much information to process needing to flow or risk monsters slipping under the bed once again while new blood interjects above. Poorly lacking of cohesive thought can't stem the tide of discontent for what must be a vile malcontent- else why the silent vitriol? How did I earn this run? Which scissors snipped the cord? Apathetic desires are unresponsive to approach. Blackened soil is next in line but is, in fact, the basis for surgical removal of color reception. Ravens barking at the moon accompanied by a symphony of caws from the dogs of war- ultimate being the true impetus for the soliloquy as seems the case more often than not. Erstwhile revolting portrait has repaired its ugly portrayal leaving few options but to take it to the page which itself shies from the task. Scheduling demands are few and far between by choice which isn't always the best cut. Open and shut case isn't quite sealed from public view. Caught in the act is in seclusion with the act until history goes on display. Infantile gesture could be just the offload needed to get a broader plan in motion though shedding lost moons' eternal glow is a flaky consideration when wearing knitted fabric or Velcro surrogates. Smothered humanity to break-down with tradition for a moment as long as nobody's looking. Attraction wilts with summer deserts. Agonized mourning is waking for another run at just mediocre. Three strikes calling me off though I clock the ump ensuring another turn at bat if time allows which is highly unlikely but for its abject probability. Refusing to honor thy silent instruction is held in contempt while coffers full of end product of job well done gets no consideration due to fear of emotional contagion. Recreated unacknowledged infliction of deep gashes is man dropped upon Venus to the clutches of a frenzied protest though it was a revised flight path to which I wasn't privy. Sensitive skin is getting a ration of shit from mercenary sources. Familiarity breeding love is missing the cliché. Standing to follow is a ballast quickly losing pounds- screwing up equilibrium though eternal quest for balance is in the heated basement next to perspiring spandex. Loading-dock implications suggest unchecked boxes. Divining a point in sign language is an easy way out though not indicative of heartfelt candor rather tongue tied around two poles. Driving home the freeze. Murdering the endorsement. Beating a red headed step-horse long after administration of embalming fluid in an advance copy of the grand finale which is anything but a work of art though performance skits are the new rage of which I have nary a clue as to why it's aimed at me. It raises periscope with each breach of the surface or reflection served straight up. One should never disrespect fine whiskey with ice or change labels without full disclosure however presumption of a passing grade is shaky at best. Self indulgent crown of thorns without implicating biblical reference. Making a case for agoraphobic misanthropic misogyny while staring at a lurid airbrush of the Madonna. While sleeping off pills that repel the venom-comatosed though fully aware of the rustling between the sheets transmuted to bloodshot but I haven't that luck.

No Reprieve

Inconsistent audit results crating the records for a second opinion. Unlikely offshoot will blow a gasket of crocodile tears or simply bury the hatchet in memory for reconsideration at a future point in time though it remains to be seen as to whether there's enough left. In the lurch of silent betrayal is skimming fingertips on a million gusts in the trades though is tapped out of requests under freedom for information which will never be freely disclosed but for bargain rack disinformation receiving the short end of the deal. Story of bad choices slated to hit autumnal airwaves has been moved forward in the lineup as splayed entrails attracted the best Nielsen ratings in beta-testing so there is no time like the present. Wildfires raining upon parades coasting down ascending stairs to a different dimension though calculation of the area will require revisit of higher math which doesn't readily accept sarcastic guests. On reprieve from giving a fuck has been ordered back to work by outside influences without consideration of exhausted pride. Scribbling illegible anecdotes is a dog with a tale to tell. Stumble on rock is sizzling in glass or shredding feet firmly implanted in a smile that's frowning- blocking any chance at comprehensible retort. Another poor solution to long term issue of hope for scintilla of peaceful terrain is good grounds for dismissal despite regulations to the contrary. Diving deeper into a place that should never be entered alone is dangerously mistaking experience for impervious. Stolen fantasy clobbered three times to Sunday. High-school musical marquee is singing far off key which once had pitch-perfect intonation. Unbelieving fallacy of kind genetics raising human ire with allusions to inexorable however ghastly preconditions. Wallowing in ill-conceived departure from basic foundation regretting decision for leeway derived from compromise which is a step in the wrong direction from either side of the logistician's table to which tethers are octopods of far reaching influence. Mendicant type forgiveness is really just a beggar's banquet with no flowers adorning the buffet. Captured in a web of my own conspiracy. Maze of misguided intention whose professional chaperon flew the coop at the first sign of border incursion. Customs can't integrate inbound traffic with a faulty control tower. Principled inclinations unheeded are chasms in morality or incoming grief. Commencement speeches falling on deaf ears. Termination papers delivered by electronic means doused in ambiguity. Nervous breakdown splintering newly discovered mines of transparent obscurity with a softer world view. Pending collapse receiving final stamp of patent approval.

This Is The End

"she gives me her cheek when i want her lips."

~dave alvin
fourth of july

A billowing accordion stoking extinguished breaths wearing dishonest Sunday best for church of a new disciple. Intuitive meditation telling more of the story than is expressed in tangible terms. Corralling logic into a manageable pen where it once roamed unbound. Likely overestimating paranoid reflection though parallax isn't easy to catch an angle on. Camping out on serious topics has a thorn in its side. Mexican Coke is popping bubbles and adding sugar to spicy mariachis strumming Tejano while pending riptide conspicuously sneaks through the crowd with tiger shark undulation and pearl smile. Networking facial before unwitting competitor who had had no competition- hence was permanently blinded by the checkered flag. Start time seems to have gone off before all drivers were revved up to pile onto pole position- some didn't even see the race for the track under their noses. Stinging reflux repeats at the attestation. Drowning in more stimulant and weed to keep up this charade of repair past bedtime. Inconsequential rumination of lost in his own head nearing solipsistic denial of your existence. Odd familiarity with the concept, albeit inverted, as the creation of your only perspective chimes in on cowbells in the middle of a city street or postcard from hell. Death taxes and singularly unique eternal loyalty are certain and the last was just deleted from the list furthering the studies of my theory on human waste of the one collective that matters and is entirely too human to boot. And currently none matter nor even exist in my whistling wheeze- froth mouthed into a pool of tears at loss of the final infinitesimal notion that tried and true holds up its end of the bargain though I wager I've long ago lost any compulsion to implicate myself in elevating any gods let alone the ones that aren't real- a planetary condition and I can't even control me. Supporting data is plastered on the walls with sputum spackle and bloody prints. Cackling processor won't stop chiming off. Going manic though I've yet to be diagnosed with the condition. Most powerful force in the universe taking its train to the second which is often mistaken for the first but they're easily confused and likely interchangeable at that. Hormone or whore-moan equivalent of chicken and egg or cart and horse propositions. The dark crevice of redemption which so quickly can lack redemptive assessment. Sitting in dire straits delivered from urge to carve initials from subsequent by an inanimate box named after poison fruit which seems at least credible if not spot on reenactment. Frozen embrace gets hot and catches terminal melt. Everything's a contradiction. I'll always miss you more than I despise you in this raw moment though maintenance of sanity is offering partial reprieve to carry-on in a negotiated deal which snags honesty in a sting operation.

Shutdown

Closing door on new relationships though surely that will irritate fates still chafing over surfeit last declarations; tiring of my overplayed b-sides. Uprooted fraction taking solo flights to the next degree won't amount to much. A bicycle made for two has only one wheel- leaking too much into concealed format which is readily unencrypted but for attention deficit order of the generation- name to be determined upon regression to chaos, straightening Nietzsche's bent back to natural pose. Cascading visions of sweat lodges are waking up in winter lakes offering no spiritual clarification. Battalion of wits preparing for a fight in which it chooses not to engage but fears a scathing report may be obliged for resolution which is the formal way of saying closure but I refuse new-age patois in deference to increasing numbers and general principle. Leaning downwind of aggression isn't a posture I've long possessed but sunspots are becoming a more relevant part of the deteriorating exterior. Spurning lucid for moment's respite is hitting all the wrong letters in rash decision which itches woeful remorse though isn't quite sure. Incompatible with former pedestal is taking a giant step downward. Void of conscience for nothing is real if I don't say so though objective inclinations are elusive properties to level. Displaying willingness to evade mass confusion is jacking polar opposites into a mad frenzy with cruel floes. Taking all into account is attempting forgiveness but cardiac aqueducts are occluded and can't take a hike in the pressure. Reaching for shooting stars but can only grab a piece before dropping under the disapproving light which sends me into hiding until someone cuts the power that will never rest in my hands if it rests at all. Interspersed disconnect is settling for a more consistent schedule to fill up the calendar in defensive repositioning. Catapulting reverie is slaughtered hope. Outlets for absolution are few and far between when the answer is always no- no matter how or in which direction my genuflection. Sedated into meteoric crater stressing over what's coming up. Cancelled into ex'd out for good which must be my doing yet I can't find the fault line- simply some minor splits. Seated with more than one is getting a bit claustrophobic. Some fears comprehend dusty biographies beyond utilitarian mastery. Is a spinning whirlwind of captions within the horror-comics appropriate for any age? Is that closed door sealed fate or simply hardheaded ignorance of colloquialism which is bound to repeat itself evermore no matter the raining laughter from above in spite of no trust in compasses anyway? Can't determine what side of the equator I rest without watching the commode flush away any inquiry. Or is that just an emanation of my own manhandled perspective? Looking for new music is caught between death rock and opera. Certain choices are a coin flip. Always call tails in hopes that's all I see as the door shuts in the mourning.

Same Grounds-Different Cup

Finding difficulty capturing stars and rerouting solar orbits. Uniting broader range to include both blue and red is mostly spent. Indisputable is need to keep diddling else risk implosion which at least would shield spectators from the gore. An unreturned envelope is circling my thoughts- agreement to demand or washing hands of situation? Legalese 101- don't ask what you don't already know. Sticking with that as long as the declaration isn't interrupted by streaming deliveries from the same destinies I've relentlessly bashed by another name of late. Purportedly dry prose is actually drowning in its obfuscation. I'd like to stare into a calm waters and see something worth the squint- perhaps an apparition which shows a better outcome than can be garnered by the vile cracks in the facade. Complicity, by definition, is explicative of a quantity equal to or greater than two, barring multiple voices throwing their ventriloquism into the same poem so why I'd weave a pointed cap is uncertain. Indecipherable can be really hard to make out. Would appreciate additional insertion of it ain't my problem anymore but I'm stuck in a quagmire that is kindly stuffed under grizzly fangs and even she can't snap me out of it so I'm relying on faith in division of responsibility however I'm not sure what that means. Chewing on soul candy over a campfire or wood floor- whichever comes first- is getting bitter. Smokey ain't here and his supplication is lost on my lighter which is heavily relied upon. Interference in distant events is a click and dip away into a class of binary hell from which I've sworn eternal truancy. Endeavor to avoid redundancy however situational demands are tightly focused at the moment which leads to repetitive motive depravity committed upon the page which is trying to get out but needs to swear adherence to drug regimen. Stripped and searched is quick process when the emperor already has no robe. Disparate hypotheticals meet where studies are conducted behind security doors making quite an uncompromising slam against the brick. On the canvas can be best option for artistic revelation. Ice doesn't heal missing screws in the erector set however. Toughing it out. Manning up. Keeping a stiff upper lip. Chin off chest. Bullshit. Stuff it in your platitude. Occupation with rendering silk from sow is keeping the bottle tabled though it has been silent since last tip of the cap regardless. Long haul trucking to no more can't help but to think there's additional yet the words flee in haste before I can spit them up. Splitting headache is picking sides. Crapping out before end of run is close to taking all the chips off the table- optimistic ones anyway. Skeptical pay-offs are always diminutive as once the count has been completed there is nothing but zero left on the ledger. Under three scoops is less than. Nothing to nothing. Tending to wither by the day. Feeding demons in the dark. Painting the cosmos red. Alone but for the arguments dogging me since I took an ill-advised stroll inside.

Slow Reclining Step To Higher Plane

Putting a premature cork in a bottle with an invisible message never written but for in crawl spaces above however sent into the tempestuous white-capped blue nevertheless. Scribe magic trick fooling no one but the other entities permeating the dew falling sweetly in the morning and perhaps a whale of a tale that breaches migrating surfaces. Jasmine blooming as automated porch lights secure the premises. Reinvigorated has yet to find a line to grip though is doing its best on the chalkboard. Slowly easing butterfly effect tying gastric system in fluttering knots. Trying to write myself out in the first act though that ship is twenty five hundred miles offshore and forty four revolutions about the crimson sun. She'll pass with stones that break free from purchase which is costly excursion yet sooner better than later although I could've used something more than a headline reiterating danger when hiking unsteady oil shale and slicked back doo under a velvet fedora. Clasping to din of hollow musings while forgetting everything that happened. Nascent glow of departing phantom is taking birth. Replaced actuators checked the wrong box on the job application. Statistical anomaly is proving the new norm. Casting call is being returned with spiked chum. Inebriated silence is unheard music thumping present distance into old persona. Strutting up refinished streets which once held a beautiful patina. Environmental awareness has no clue as to atmospheric readings. Pain of hindsight is looking for a witch named hazel yet nothing's doing but steel wool which will have to do in lieu of discounted for lack of supply which is counterintuitive on its face however abundance and demand are suspended between regulatory loopholes wide as abandoned wells of logical standards that play during opening credits that get none. Shrieking into a slasher film reel to add gravitas while covering my ears with splayed fingers. Glaring into an eclipse while pleading for sight. Reprised refrain is old news which could have emanated from Olympus or the good book struggling with questionable morality if taken at face value which is judging text by deceptively becoming countenance. Creeping into more knowledge is no longer part of the strategy given a dismal track record which would rather hurdle over anything I create despite plethora of failure within confined dialogue. Smoker's cough is in the sink. I wrapped a body in a bag- sending the skeleton packing. Onetime catastrophic incident taken with innocuous substitute. Contemplating contempt through transparent rose lips I stole from a wicked garden. Or so I call it to allay inadequate assessments in overexposed imagery.

Farewell Goddess Of The Hunt

Theoretical caveman instinctive response factor raised on a mainsail and perhaps a mystery solved. No direction can't find its way. Better off without a wives' tale never actually got hitched. Unconcerned posting has termite swarm superfluously interested but hardened shell refuses petitionary advances. Time for change is counting quarters in terms of hours but it's really just another day. Unaccompanied visits to the wishing well has nothing good to say about goldfish in the bowl but then might be expecting too much carnival. Sign sealed delivered is loud and clear as the bay blasting Coltrane winds through audiophile hi-fi. Unresolved stations find a place to air complaints in new format without participant-be-advised type histrionic attachments. Unspecified issue is a certain topical amalgam yet to be delivered-if at all, due to lack of inertia or simply not rocking the horse that laid the golden egg. Remorse is looking for penance though absolution is in action while deed may be transferred elsewhere. Unretractable motion may set a new round of negotiations into play despite scuttled shots at reconciliation due to disagreements on direction of ground floor blueprints tearing through twelve bars with calloused fingers as gospel doves depart the chorus line. Best intention is given consequence of axiomatic relevance and thinnest margin of error though isn't pleased with reciprocal motivation. Calculated risks are perilous snaps on a broken abacus. Vying for attention is pained absence. Irretrievable dream, figment of vain optimism. Taking my lumps in accordance with union guidelines which sometimes include infantile tantrums though needing one's diapers changed is no basis for commingling affairs. Complicating mannerisms is undefined existential arrow in a quiver shaking the palms of hollow husks. Giving into spin the bottle ruled by unfaltering swerve of multi-dash philosophy is landing on it doesn't matter anymore- there's nothing to see here but the bones- move along. Encouraging a final kiss off into secreting chef special should have relied upon scrabble education rather than jeopardize the stew by braining ingredients- a dish best served cold and never to be reliable without confirmation from both sides. Stepping stones to softer flooring is a foot forward. Fortunate is an empty inbox as the outflow stumbles wildly but accomplishes little in throwing up a white flag. Already spoken can't be unheard- rattling incessant. Malice's talking but might well have been a slithering Pentecostal line getting the call- I have no app for translation. Surreal ram-rod stuffs metaphysical comprehension above logical explanation which is offered no call-back after the audition. Nobody left to blame is letting me have it with my own weapons. No nirvana in heaven is hell. No longer in need is carved in primeval walls where the club hangs and the hunter falls to his eponymous Roman goddess. Fields plowed to a dustbowl where green once blanketed like snow. So who can blame her? Not entirely honest rhetoric has no alternative. Bound quickly to the first soaring plane to free. Send a postcard, baby. I've never been.

It's All Over Now Red White And Blue

Journey to end of line taking shape in formless narrative for that's the mangrove which feeds the bats despite linear disavowal. Cows jumping over stars while herders chew cud. Raindrops dancing off a moonlit hood hitting warp speed at the speed of light yet it's not clear if it's just repeating itself on the lonesome e-highway or adding nouns for the sake of the song. Scattered remnants of lives destroyed by inattention to detailed accounts stuck in post-war boxes thieving intuition its natural oils. Despair in mascara reigns chemo-denervation parties with so much collagen that botox is called for emergency repair. Youth consuming hormonal imbalance growing facial hair impervious to shaving its innocence. Rejected dejected downtrodden interrupted by brief interludes with chemical elation or climactic revelry while jasmine casts sweet into sour miasma. Familiarity with my breed negates further communication with communal flag-bearers who now know my real name. Narcissus is still waiting for respect though the green room is filled with higher priority. Gilded mountains oxidize. Trojan horses lead a charge through the gates while grating rejection douses traditional construct with spontaneous combustion as the alligators are wrestled to exhaustion shutting down the moat until further notice. Red herrings fished from bread crumb streams hoping for resolution before fatal proves its theory. Engines that can't. Chaos that is. Order stuck in entropy bound and tethered with riddle inside allegorical reference points which struggle to maintain the metaphor ascending to the heavens unless you're looking up in which case it's down. Hustlers pimp soulless to meet eternal damnation head-on. Empires inevitably collapse- leaving paper trails for future generations who decry deforestation on petroleum scrawled poster board which once reached for the light so that lichen could live. Nero's fiddling again shunning Daniels in favor of Manson who makes more sense than a tree full of owls inside a box of squirrels. Betsy Ross sits in a grave behind concertina wire sponsored by the UN. Heaving sulfuric stench of rockets' deafening red glare can choke a whore. Emotional content lost within a jam of ether traffic sucking interpersonal its last handwriting. Indescribable love searching for meaning while slaughtering butterfly effect with an anvil. Holding back tears of eviscerated expectation but they tell us to carry forward for the sake of overwhelmed surface area lacking space to sustain withering organic fallacy or just grab a smile and watch your fears melt into Hindu baptisms in waters too deep from which to crawl. Depressive OCD with hints of ADHD wants its MTV. Disorders without breath can never die if eastern mystics are flipped on their backs. Slapping inappropriate conjecture atop a scrap heap which could be treasure to flies starving on emaciated landing strips. A magic carpet flies over Mesopotamia after summoning a jury of peers wishing to hear a viable explanation for logical incongruence. Genies are rubbing themselves out of lamps that fail to throw white sparks as the sands drift to denominator. Absurd taken to nth degree after failing a polygraph following the third. Bases under siege by sentient wonder-lust which has no passion for intellectual purview of philistine territories that capture the lines but can't see art for the letters AWOL from stochastic models trying to solve for derivatives adding up to some momentum yet still can't turn over the motor. Checkered table cloths are towels wrapped around jihad which could be marginally politically incorrect however dropping obviating prefix sums itself up nicely at origin axes which is just long-winded allusion to nothing. Branching out in stagnant ridicule of canon bursting which isn't much of a limb to deflower. Wandering old streets through banal designs conspicuously placed over rejected history. Bytes of the apple carry electric reek of 1939 Berlin sterilized by nannies standing short behind tall troops promising better world for us all if you just drink this. Careful what you wish for is now a single keystroke. Defrocked habits could use another big bang despite doctrine forbidding the science. Inescapable floods of mundanity tying their way to the top while constricted vessels are lost in vapid effort too close to the reflection within holographic visions of counterpoised mirrors in which they live. Mobs roam to each other's side for affirmation of mutual existence before offing one another with human condition that is spreading like a roofied prom queen wildfire. Cascading boulders too heavy for Greek tragedy and Romans burning to a crazed fiddle after sage warnings die in inferno pining of a madman who was anything but. Meetings at crossroads unheeded by counterparties with alabaster smiles barely obscuring pointed intent. Doves losing shine after sailing through the rafters of faith where none exists are ratted out as pigeons that flew the coop. Engorged central powers forever in bulk-up phase nourished by ignorance which can't see peril of feeding wild-beasts- concisely written on walls stretching back to a another blip on cosmic clocks into caves where hieroglyphics sufficed for art of war before that of word- though what difference would it make if genetics hold to Darwin like round to Galileo or Aristotle? Supposed heretics slain at stakes by masses of grocery clerks and errand boys as delineated in jungle-rot patois- graphic cinematic oration of atrocity delivered by obesity refusing elevation to red carpets drenched in blood but remaining high on propped exaltation tasting nothing like pulp. Generations stripped of drive-ins and happy endings in deference to conspicuous consumption fully supported by intelligence agencies who lack any but find ways around crack in the ghetto before studying dada as a second language for suppressive fire. Classes derided for long-division of ledgers which never balance nor ever will. Rugs pulling rooms together unwoven with pitchy vocals. Wandering without haste through Gila tracks in expansive desert relegating pharaohs to the heavy lifting while allowing bread time to levitate on seething boulders. Dead Sea is really just sick but trinket sales would plummet if the truth got out. Fallen from the cross read back to front is imparting another story which twists the theme but not spirit. Zeitgeist is terminal. Jacaranda bloom violet over whitecaps which throw charlatan and pious from the kingdom which is quite possibly a conspiracy among gods colluding to net the waves so outsiders remain as is but catch surfeit innocents in the soppy entanglements. Spiders stomped reappearing in droves to watch inexorable stampede of allegedly more foul creations- themselves just looking to make it home. Where the heart is follows the head everywhere so nobody knows if there really is a landing point for rustling treetops unable to steady even in deadest of silent nights- theorizing what they see before the only reality that counts but nobody's keeping score. Spike talon eagle's landing on your front doorstep and tossed like a newspaper at European disunion just to solidify counterpoints to one world one people. Napalm Sundays are coming down with a hard rain. Somehow karmic realignment gave the limbs back to kids' books but got lost on a bet and branches are rapidly reallocated whence they came. Mustangs leaping barbs before hooked into last breath take shelter on a mesa free from malice of poor-thought. Man's inhumanity to man and anything within earshot erecting misanthropic demons out of kind pallbearers holding the casket of genetic miscoding. Selfish disconnect from selfless is nonstarter though the bullpen is full of relief yet gastric imbroglios never cease to report- especially evident in off-seasons of disconnect. When I was seventeen it wasn't a very good year. When I was twenty one I dealt myself a poor hand against a strong house and the cards collapsed with unfortunately chosen words. Old blue eyes are baggy as corner drugstores. A lionized rose garden is planted in Camelot which can't dig itself out from a round table built on crooked trappings like a pregnancy terminated in a drunken pool. Ironic implication skipping syllables to avoid connection. Hermetic voices stuck in solipsistic blindness that might just see too well if taken with a grain of objective. Envisioning better place in time is falling off atlas-shrugs at notion that everything is circular 'cuz the weight is becoming overbearing- displacing concern for glorified philosophical dissertation however convincing. A broad-sword hangs over the collective head of the indecisive collective which has gathered at the front door but can't reach a common solution that won't part splitting hairs. Sound of music is bumping a six-four on thirteens around a corner on three. Chasing white rabbits with barrels of monkeys kicking back to china shops where the bulls are having a bear of a time negotiating tightly strung ligatures taking themselves all too seriously until plunging to potters' fields dotting the landscape with soldiers unknown to even themselves. Rats in the cellar are caged behind bars without so much as spinning wheel. Overreaching interventionists who took a rap for tapping against the drunken grain and several capitol pages side-step the line with their backs against the wall. Dissention nipped at the bud of something original so anachronism can nurture status quo. Flea market snake-oil pawned off as scripture due to singed edges. Atheists showing porcelain icons how it's done. Church bells ringing funeral dirges years before taken off life support. Only good clown is a dead clown 'less he's fending off Brahmas. Santa delivers bombshells in July but paralysis sets in and the unfaithful foxhole is loaded with a circular genuflection so no path to god is ignored just in case. Masticating vultures eating carrion which regurgitates lead as a consolation prize though no condolences are extended. Apex predators are muting the clock-tower from the bottom rung. Sun is bringing darkness to the day where it will die in the shadows of grey cities with questionably white streets and ivory towers with conspicuous black marks which play rubes for bigger and better though unfulfilled expectations grow on Italian marble. Tumbleweeds two-step it on heartache tar which never sands the plane quick enough to avoid waking to pantomimed nightmares- torturing- no matter the crosses and silver bullets wetted with holy water tossed down range. Skies part for flying apes over poppy fields and tripping mice conduct orchestras in g-rated adultery which is really a misdirect of grammar but all papers are in order for my license. Playing connect the dots in hopes for a renewed sense of yesterday but tomorrow won't move aside for today. Some yesterdays are more equal than others anyway. Wafting cancer dancing into retrograde and the world in my head collapses. Korean drivers proving cliché is a reasoned reply to factionalized invective carrying malodorous explication of still-life careening through intersections. The bins are full of loons which prefer mountainside lakes but can't see past Thorazine daze long enough to analyze the psychotic diagnosis and while the months stoned in a crowded pond. Thor slams thunderclaps at trailer parks with vengeance before bolting to roofing nails which is another aisle heard from looking to boost revenue figures. A vortex of lullabies passes with strawberry scents and temporary respites in face of the inanity which is absurd on its face but so much for sticky calculus thrown at numb dentures rotting at the core of poison fruit whose suggested aphrodisiacal qualities are contagion in the oasis growing modest in fig leaves which have too much sugar for the aforementioned nanny but smugglers are making bank. Acronyms have taken over the drones which go on and on. Full fledged battle is campaigning for lighter sentencing while pickled legislators sip beam who's in possession of a very persuasive spotlight. Anonymous blessings are mixed bags. Declarative statements have the fates rolling out of their seats when the music's over and you don't have to go home but can't stay here. Sirens break the trains chugging into the arms of the sandman who knows you'll be back. Strange sensation is fatalist with a smile. Loathing kindred genetics with a dollar in a cup is apparently not gonna crash St. Peter's party anytime before pederasts who never miss a seventh day confessional- hailing Mary's little lamb in the ensuing Mardi Gras which can't give up lechery for lent and all is forgiven. Seeing death through rose colored glasses protecting sight from Styx while a trident waits patiently for sin. Thanking wrong-doers for benediction which utilize deep cover- invisible but for manifestation of results. Standardized tests are substitute examinations. The oaks know my name and have accepted apologies for initial disregard. Liana snaking up lattices to break with whitewashed tradition. The tunes with chops ride against prevailing currents. Decline of civilization on the doorstep sure as firewater ignites with reservation. Certain as roosters crowing unsyncopated biorhythmic discrepancies. Counting eggs before they hatch yet finding some do. Cries in the dark are empty voids. Promises, more like if the mood fits. Black jacket hiding gracefully aging pastel basics still lays out fundamental realities when approached with malice. Death knell imminent once the piano learns player's braille but stars still streak above. Hundreds of dead dreams are a flock of ravens cawing sideways glances as aggressive mews emanate from corralled populous stuck to red tape until the adhesion wears and yellow supplants while supplicant mothers scream in horror. But the seals still bark as

SEALs grunt and jungle gyms delight iphone cams. Casual observation will lead to formal inquiry and find me in contempt because I hold it to be self evident. Castles slip back to jagged rocks which roll and collect all the mossy implications on the way down. Eventually the jazz finds resolution within common theme of a silent plot- six feet under or just waiting to get there.

The End

About the author:

Danny was raised in L.A. in a storm of turmoil that landed him right in the middle of the 80's punk rock scene as a wild teen in the streets. He would move to New York and transform himself into a successful mover and shaker on Wall Street; years later developing his innate talent for writing as a way to balance the intensity and duality of his existence. His first book of poems, Fractured, released in 2012, was the first book published by Punk Hostage Press.

Danny's work has been published in Paraphilia Magazine, The Examiner, Edgar Allan Poet library and The Nervous Breakdown, The Nexxuss and Deep Tissue among numerous other publications and e-zines. Additionally, Danny was included in a chap, The Musophobist, with three other poets, published by Unadorned Press. Back in Los Angeles, he continues to push forward with multiple writing projects in the making.